# THE FERAL FOLKLORIST

### VOLUME 1

## HAUNTINGS, HEXES, AND THE CURSED SOUTH

### GREGORY LEE WHITE
as told by Papa Gee

White Willow Press
Nashville, TN

The Feral Folklorist, Volume 1
Hauntings, Hexes, and the Cursed South
by
Gregory Lee White
as told by Papa Gee

Text:
Gregory Lee White

Cover Art & Illustrations:
Gregory Lee White

First Edition 2025

Published by
White Willow Press
211 Donelson Pike, Suite 111
Nashville, Tn 37214

Printed in the United States

ISBN: 978-1-965586-08-2

# TABLE OF CONTENTS

*A Wicked Little Podcast*
www.feralfolklorist.com

# OTHER BOOKS BY GREGORY LEE WHITE

Clucked – The Tale of Pickin Chicken

Making Soap from Scratch: How to Make Handmade Soap – A Beginners Guide and Beyond

Essential Oils and Aromatherapy - How to Use Essential Oils for Beauty, Health, and Spirituality

Little House Search – A Puzzle Book and Tour of the Works of Laura Ingalls Wilder

The Use of Magical Oils in Hoodoo, Prayer, and Spellwork

Papa Gee's Hoodoo Herbal - The Magic of Herbs, Roots, and Minerals in the Hoodoo Tradition

The Stranger in the Cup – How to Read Your Luck and Fate in the Tea Leaves by Gregory Lee White and Catherine Yronwode

How to Use Amulets, Charms, and Talismans in the Hoodoo and Conjure Tradition
by Catherine Yronwode and Gregory Lee White

Lenormand Basics – How to Read Lenormand Cards for Beginners

Casting Love Spells – Rituals of Romance, Passion, and Attraction

Hex Appeal – How to Cast Dark Spells of Revenge, Cursing, and Damnation

Fairy Lore and Myths

Papa Gee's Book of Candle Magic

Cernunnos – The Lord of Wild Things

Hecate – The Goddess of Witchcraft

The Sacred Phallus – Magical Symbol of Power and Protection

The Folklore of Plants: Botanical Spells and Rituals

Tarot Magic: Spells, Spreads, and Sorcery Using the Tarot Deck

# INTRODUCTION

We've always tried to keep what we fear sealed—under floorboards, behind plaster, or buried deep enough inside ourselves that no one would find it. When fear couldn't be hidden, we named it. A hex. A haint. Bad blood. We blamed the wind, or the old woman at the edge of town, or the Devil waiting at a crossroads. That's the work folklore does: it gives shape to what we can't explain and a ritual to contain it.

For me, that work started early. I was thirteen when I began reading books about real hauntings—true ghost stories, restless spirits, anything that hinted the world might be larger than adults would admit. I wasn't drawn to monsters or gore. I liked the quiet kind of haunting, the Hitchcock sort, where the air feels off and the house remembers all the horrible things that happened there. That taste never left. It was less about fear and more about proof—proof that the world had things hidden underneath that most people either can't see or won't acknowledge.

By my twenties, my life took an unexpected turn, and I became a nightclub performer. That stage taught me discipline. It taught me how to read a room, how to pace a story, and how to hold silence long enough that it started working for you instead of against you. Every night was a study in rhythm, attention, and energy—the same tools any storyteller or conjure worker uses, just under brighter lights. What I learned there about presence and timing would later shape how I teach, how I write, and even how I work magic.

Offstage, I was still chasing what moved beneath the surface. My interests turned from ghost stories toward the living traditions that gave them life. I studied folk religions and real magic, learning that belief isn't just theory—it's infrastructure. I found out that most magical workers practiced in kitchens and gardens, not temples. Their altars were stove tops, their offerings practical. That world felt familiar because it echoed what I'd already known growing up.

I come from the Western Kentucky coal region, what folks sometimes call the "cousin region" to Appalachia. We were close enough to hear the old stories and pick up the habits, even if we didn't always know where they came from. People there understood signs and omens, how to stop blood with words, and how to keep a garden safe from envy or harm. Nobody called it witchcraft, and nobody called it religion. It was just what you did because your people always had. Later I learned that much of it came from what others call granny magic—the work of women who kept both home and spirit together when there wasn't much else to rely on. From them I learned that a broom can guard a doorway, a candle can stand in for a prayer, and a story can heal if you tell it with care.

Tarot entered my life the same way—quietly, through curiosity. The cards never felt like fortune-telling to me; they felt like conversation. They taught me to listen for pattern and possibility, to see how stories repeat themselves until we learn what they're trying to say. Reading cards and reading folklore turned out to be the same skill in different languages. Both rely on attention to symbols, both depend on respect, and both ask for humility before meaning.

In 1999, my husband and I opened our metaphysical store, aromaG's Botanica, and we've been part of that world ever since. The tools, the spells, the herbs, the stories—they've never been hobbies. They're the language of a life lived between the mystical and the practical. I've written books on folk magic and spellcraft, taught classes, and worked with people looking for answers you won't find in the mainstream. You listen, you interpret, and you help make sense of what someone already knows but can't yet name.

Over time, those paths began to cross—folklore, conjure, storytelling, performance, and the Appalachian magic I grew up around—and *The Feral Folklorist* grew naturally out of them. The podcast became a way to gather everything in one place: the history, the hauntings, my writing, and the practical knowledge that comes from years of reading cards and working magic. The microphone simply replaced the front porch. The stories stayed the same.

# DEDICATION AND ACKNOWLEDGMENTS

This book exists because people kept listening. *The Feral Folklorist* started as a podcast—half history, half haunting, recorded early in the morning with coffee and a script—and it grew because you showed up for every story. You wrote, you shared, you asked questions, and you reminded me that folklore still has a place at the table.

To everyone who tuned in from the beginning, who passed the episodes along, or who left a message saying a story had followed you into your own thoughts—thank you. You're the reason this work keeps expanding.

What began as a single show became the start of a whole world: The Folkoreum online magazine, the essays, the classes, the Youtube videos on folktales and ghost stories, the books—they all grew out of your curiosity and your belief that old stories still matter. You proved that folklore doesn't fade. It adapts.

To the listeners, readers, patrons, and friends who've kept the fire steady: your attention is the one magic that never fails.

# THE DEVIL AT THE CROSSROADS

They still say the Devil waits at the crossroads. Folks have seen him or claim they did—leaning on a fence post, hat pulled low, smiling like he already knows the deal you're about to make. Every version points to one name in the end. Robert Johnson.

He was born in 1911 in Hazlehurst, Mississippi—Black, poor, and ambitious in a world that punished all three. The South didn't offer much that led anywhere worth walking. Field work and mill work were steady, but steady didn't mean you'd get anywhere in life.

Music was one of the few trades that could make a difference. A man who could play well and entertain people usually had plenty to eat, could travel, and find some form of independence. Johnson started with the harmonica and did all right with it. But when he picked up a guitar, people noticed for the wrong reasons. His rhythm wobbled, his slide scratched, and the older musicians told him, kindly as they could, that maybe he wasn't cut out for it.

Then he was gone. Not long enough to disappear, but long enough for questions to take root. When he came back, his playing had changed in a way no one could explain. His hands no longer fumbled. His chords were clean, his runs effortless, and his slide carried the ache that the blues was built to hold. It sounded like he had been taken apart and put back together by something that understood sound from the inside out. The change was so complete that practice seemed too small to explain it. People said he must have gone down to a certain crossroads after dark and made a trade. The story settled fast: a man dressed in black met him there, took his guitar, tuned it, played one song, and handed it back. From that night on, Robert Johnson played like no one else alive.

No one ever agreed on where it happened. Some pointed to the crossing of Highways 61 and 49 in Clarksdale. Others swore it was deeper in the Delta at a place that can't be found unless a person really needs it. The only thing everyone agreed on was that something had changed, and that change defied reason.

Later accounts put Johnson's missing months in Arkansas, studying under Ike Zimmerman—a guitarist who practiced late at night in the family graveyard because it was quiet there. That explanation satisfies historians, but it never caught on with the people who had heard him play. Technical skill could not account for what his sound became.

Myth explained it better than fact, and Johnson seemed to know it. He understood that the truth of a story often lives in how it's told, not in what's recorded. He leaned into that legend. The proof is in his own songs, where the bargain was never confessed outright but can still be heard between the lines.

During the few short years he performed, Robert Johnson recorded twenty-nine songs that shaped what would become modern blues and, later, rock music. He played anywhere that would let him set up—street corners, juke joints, logging camps, small halls, and house parties. In 1938, at twenty-seven, he drank whiskey that had been poisoned, most say by a jealous husband, and died soon after. He was buried in an unmarked grave. The story didn't end there. It stayed alive because it answered a question that reason never could—how a man with nothing more than a guitar and his will could come back from obscurity with music that sounded far older than he was.

## THE HISTORY

In West and Central African cosmology, the crossroads is not a place of danger but a point of exchange. It functions as a boundary where the physical and spiritual worlds intersect, allowing communication between them. It is not a metaphor. It is a real location, understood as one of the primary access points to divine or ancestral presence. Energy passes through it, requests are carried across it, and guidance arrives because of it. The logic behind this is structural, not poetic. When movement is required, it happens through a place already shaped for it.

In Yoruba tradition—one of the most intact African spiritual systems to survive the transatlantic slave trade—that role belongs to Eshu, also known as Legba or Eleggua depending on region or diaspora. He is the gatekeeper, the messenger, the interpreter between human beings and the divine. He maintains the border between worlds, and no contact with the orisha or other spirits begins without first acknowledging him. Offerings left for him at the crossroads aren't bribes or bargains. They're gestures of respect. Some bring rum, coins, candy, or tobacco—small indulgences meant to please him, to coax him into listening.

When Africans were enslaved and forced into the Americas, they carried these understandings with them. They did not abandon their gods; they adjusted how they spoke to them. What had been open practice became discreet. Figures once called by name were hidden behind the faces of saints. Offerings became household customs. Rituals were folded into daily life in ways that let them survive without formal sanction. That process was not symbolic blending; it was tactical preservation.

In the American South, especially in places where Black communities had little access to organized religion or medicine, this inherited knowledge became the foundation of what is now called hoodoo. It is not a religion. It is a body of folk practice shaped by African cosmology, refined by survival, and proven through work. Within hoodoo, the crossroads kept its original role. It remained a place to make requests, to lay down spells, and to release energy—particularly energy that had stalled or turned sour. The work done there was not performance. It was maintenance.

When a spell needed to move—when a petition had been prayed over, when a baneful item had served its purpose, or when something had to be carried out of the home without being brought back in—the crossroads served as the point of disposal. The worker didn't linger. The object was buried, scattered, or dropped while walking. The common rule was to toss it over the left shoulder and keep moving without turning back. The act wasn't symbolic theater; it followed the same structural logic that defined the practice itself. If something has been sent away, you don't recall it with your attention. You don't speak to anyone on the road. You don't explain what you've done. You finish the work, and you leave.

## THE MAGIC

The belief that the crossroads was dangerous came from a different tradition altogether. In European Christian folklore, crossroads marked places of confusion or punishment. Witches were buried there so they would stay lost. Criminals were executed there to prevent their spirits from returning home. Those customs came from an old unease with liminal ground—places that were neither one thing nor another, neither church nor village, belonging to no one. Folks believed that if you met something powerful at a crossroads, it couldn't be holy. It had to be the man in black, the devil with a contract—the figure who offers power, then takes much more than he ever means to give.

That interpretation didn't come from any African belief system. It came from European fear. But stories travel faster than the truth behind them, and by the time they reached American soil, the two systems had already begun to blend. A man too talented, a woman too lucky, a child too gifted for the place they were born into—each was treated with suspicion. Their talent wasn't credited to effort or determination. It was called unnatural and meant a dark deal must have been made. That suspicion trailed Black musicians, conjure workers, midwives, seers, and root doctors well into the twentieth century. In some places, it still does.

What the crossroads offers in traditional practice isn't power without a price. In hoodoo, when someone wants to develop a skill—whether it's playing an instrument, reading cards, interpreting dreams, or praying with focus—they may be told to visit the crossroads before sunrise for seven straight days. They bring the tool of their trade with them. No speeches. No ceremony. Just showing up and doing the work. If the spirit of the place takes notice, and the request is sincere, the change begins quietly—a cleaner tone, a sharper insight, a clarity that wasn't there the week before.

That isn't a bargain. It's an acknowledgment. The crossroads carries movement, but it asks for direction. It isn't a shortcut—it's where you stand still long enough to ask the right question.

In rootwork, the crossroads has a purpose. When someone's carrying something that's done its time, or when a spell has finished and needs to be released, the crossroads gives that power somewhere to go. The goal isn't to wash it away or call it clean. It's to hand it off. The worker isn't scrubbing themselves of guilt or sin; they're shifting energy from one place to another, letting the road itself decide which way it travels next.

These days, the crossroads is mostly used for getting rid of things. That might mean name papers, candle stubs, ashes, oil-soaked cloth, the contents of a jar, broken glass, or graveyard dirt—anything that's been worked and needs a proper place to rest. It can also mean a written petition, a few words spoken into folded paper, or some small token tied to a spell that's already run its course.

If the work was meant to harm or drive something away, it's thrown over the left shoulder while walking through the crossroads, and you don't look back. If it's a petition meant to travel or send energy outward, it's buried shallow right where the paths meet. Either way, the rule's the same: walk through, release what you came to release, and head home in silence. The job isn't done until you cross your own doorstep without saying a word.

There's no need to make a show of it. The crossroads isn't a stage—it's an ending. And that clean break matters. In this kind of work, leftover energy is a real thing. If you talk about what you did, second-guess it, or glance back over your shoulder, you call it home again. The rule is simple: if you ask the road to carry it, let it go.

Offerings at the crossroads serve a different purpose. They aren't for disposal; they're for relationship. When something is left for the spirit who keeps the gate—whether you call him Eshu, Legba, or in some paths, it's Hecate who answers—it's done with care. The gift is small but chosen with respect, offered by name and with a clear request. There's no need for dramatics. If the spirit accepts, the air shifts just enough to notice. If not, the place stays quiet, and you come back another day.

Most of the confusion these days comes from people thinking the crossroads is a place for summoning. That comes from reading the Robert Johnson story too literally—turning a piece of folklore into a set of directions. Folks heard "midnight," "object," "spirit," and "power," and figured that was the recipe. But in the traditions that shaped that story, the crossroads isn't a vending machine, and spirits don't come running just because they're called. No worker raised in the old ways would ever tell someone to summon the Devil there. That's not how this works. The Devil in that story isn't a villain waiting in the dark; he's the name we give to power that comes with a price.

Real pacts do happen, but they're never casual. A pact is a standing agreement made by someone who knows what they're giving and what they're asking for. When it happens at a crossroads, it's built on relationship, not curiosity. The offerings are thoughtful, the terms stay private, and nothing about it is guaranteed. Most crossroads work, even the heavy kind, isn't about signing your soul away. It's about choosing a direction. The crossroads isn't where a bargain begins; it's where a person says their intention out loud and lets the road carry it.

The rules for the crossroads don't change much across the South. When the work is laid down, you don't look back. You don't linger. You don't pick up anything that's lying there, no matter how ordinary or tempting it looks. You don't talk to anyone on the walk home. If someone calls your name, keep walking. If a stranger steps out and asks a question, don't answer. These aren't just old superstitions— they're good boundaries. Once the work has been moved, it needs to stay moved. Doubt or distraction can pull it right back to you.

These steps aren't optional; they're part of what makes the place work. A person who treats the crossroads like a movie scene or a story prop won't get much for their trouble. The place will stay still— or worse, it'll answer in a way they didn't expect. Crossroads don't reward curiosity. They answer honesty with clarity.

## THE SIGNS

Stories about crossroads encounters are often laughed off in public and told in full detail once the lights are low. What ties them together is an unusual event. They don't usually start with someone chasing power. They start with someone just trying to get home. A road they've driven a hundred times starts to look strange. Landmarks slide out of place. The air inside the car turns heavy and still. Gravel fades beneath the tires. The clock keeps ticking, but the body stops feeling it.

In north Alabama, folks still tell one about a hunter who set out before daylight near his family's land. He'd known those woods since boyhood and could find his way without a lantern. That morning, though, he came to a four-way clearing he'd never seen. In the center stood a black rooster, still and silent, the dirt beneath it marked with a cross. When he turned to go back, nothing looked right. The trees were wrong. The woods were too quiet. His tracks were gone. When searchers found him three days later, he couldn't say where he'd been. The soles of his boots were caked with red clay from a part of the county nobody remembered him ever visiting.

In Natchez, Mississippi, there's a country cemetery where an old logging trail meets the road that runs to its gates. Right where those paths cross, folks sometimes find things laid out with care—mason jars filled with rust-colored water and grave dirt, bones tied in red flannel, doll heads packed with nails. Nobody touches them. Around there, the rule's the same as it's always been which is: what's left at the crossroads isn't yours to move.

One man broke that rule. He picked up a jar and opened it, just to see what was inside. Later, he said a heat hit the back of his skull so hard it made his vision go white. He dropped the jar, jumped in his truck, and drove home. For three nights, something walked the edge of his property. He never saw it, but he heard the steps and the sound of breathing that wasn't his. On the fourth night it stopped. He never took that road again.

Stories like that aren't told just to scare you. They're told to remind you. Liminal ground is never empty, and what's left there isn't decoration. It's about somebody's working spell and when you stepd into it, even by accident, can stir up things you don't mean to.

Another figure turns up in stories from all over: the man in black. The details shift, but the shape stays the same. He stands just off the road, always near an intersection, always still. Some say he's tall, silent, wearing a long coat even in the heat. Others say he shows up as a black dog with eyes that catch red light when there shouldn't be any. The stories usually start with car trouble or a wrong turn. He doesn't speak.

He doesn't move. He just watches. Most folks who see him drive away without harm, but something changes after—a turn in their life, a sudden sense of knowing, or a dream that comes back night after night, speaking in symbols they half understand.

These stories aren't told as miracles or warnings. They're told because they keep happening. The people who share them don't claim to understand what they saw. They only say they followed the rules. They didn't speak. They didn't turn around. They didn't reach out. And after it passed through, something that had been stuck started to move again.

When the pattern's broken, the outcome sounds the same in every version. Something lingers. Not a ghost, not a curse—just a question that won't stay quiet. That's what the crossroads gives most often. Not answers, but a nudge. It speeds up whatever's already trying to move inside you.

## THE WORK

When a person reaches the point where no road feels sure, the crossroads stops being a place of power and starts being a place of alignment. Going there doesn't hand you an answer—it opens the space to hear one. The work that follows isn't about forcing results. It's about naming the choice, asking for guidance, and clearing the path so you can move without confusion.

This spell is for those moments when you have to say

the decision out loud. It's meant for when you're on the edge of a choice—not when the plan's already made or when you've decided what you want to hear. It's for the time when reason runs out and movement won't come.

Write your petition on plain paper. Keep it simple. Name what's really in front of you: Should I leave this job? Can I trust this person? Which way am I meant to go? The paper doesn't need fancy language. It needs truth. Fold it toward you three times. Each fold draws the answer closer. Hold the paper in your hand—don't hide it in a bag or a jar. This isn't a spell for secrecy. It's a request that needs to be heard.

Timing isn't set by the moon or a calendar. It's set by readiness. Go at sunrise when you need a new direction. Go at dusk when you need to understand something before it ends. Walk to a crossroads you can reach on foot. If that's not possible, choose another in-between place—a bend where road turns to trail, or where the city gives way to open ground. The walk itself matters. Getting there is part of the work.

When you arrive, stand in the center, or off to the side if that feels safer. Hold the folded petition in one hand. Carry a small cup or jar of clean water. Bring three coins, silver if you have it, but any metal will do. Don't speak yet. Wait until your body settles enough to ask your question.

When the moment feels right, say the question out loud. Don't whisper. Don't raise your voice. Let your tone match the weight of what you're asking. Then pour the water slowly onto the dirt and say: *From this place, I ask to be seen. From this place, I ask to be guided. Let the spirits of the road carry my words where they need to go.*

The water isn't for show. It carries what you've said into the ground.

Set the coins on the dirt—not tossed, not stacked. Let each one touch earth. This isn't payment; it's acknowledgment. It says you know where you're standing, and that the place knows you too.

Bury the folded petition shallow near the coins, or right at the heart of the crossroads if the soil allows. Set a stone on top—not to seal it, but to mark that something was left there with intent. If you brought a personal object tied to the question, take it home. Keep it on your altar or work table until the answer begins to show itself.

No photos. No proof. No talking on the walk back. Go home in silence, and don't speak of it until something shifts. The answer might come as a dream, a passing phrase, or a moment of clear knowing that won't leave you alone. It may not be loud. It may not be easy. But if the crossroads heard you, and if your question was true, the movement will begin.

In folk practice, the crossroads isn't a concept to study. It's a place to meet with respect, to use cleanly, and to leave as you found it. It isn't an ending. It's a hinge. What opens afterward depends on how you asked, and whether you were ready to listen. Opening a magical door is the easy part. Having the courage to walk through it is a different story altogether.

# THE GREENBRIER GHOST WHO TESTIFIED IN COURT

They still talk about the ghost that testified in Greenbrier County. Some say it was a story meant to keep men honest. Others insist it happened exactly as the court records claim.

In January of 1897, a young woman named Elva Zona Heaster was found dead at the foot of the stairs in her home in Greenbrier County, West Virginia. She was twenty-three, recently married, and had shown no sign of illness. The official report listed the cause of death as *everlasting faint*—a phrase once used when a woman died suddenly, and no one wanted to ask why. Other accounts say the doctor claimed it was heart failure. No autopsy was performed. No questions were raised. Within two days she was buried.

Her mother, Mary Jane Heaster, refused to accept that explanation. She had never trusted Zona's husband, a man who called himself Edward but whose full name was Erasmus Stribbling Trout Shue. From the beginning she had seen his temper, and in the weeks after the wedding she had watched her daughter grow quiet. When she learned that Edward had hovered over the body, told the doctor not to touch her neck, and tied a scarf tightly around it, saying only that it was her favorite, she knew something was wrong.

Mary Jane later testified that her daughter came to her in four dreams. Each time, the message was the same. Zona's spirit told her that Edward had lost his temper after an argument over supper. That he had grabbed her by the neck and broken it. That her death had not come from faintness or illness, but from his hands. In the last dream, the spirit turned her head completely around to show what had been done. These were not symbols or impressions. Mary Jane described them as direct visits—clear, deliberate, and precise.

She carried what she had seen to the local prosecutor, John Alfred Preston. He listened, not because he believed in ghosts, but because her certainty left little room to dismiss her. Quietly, he began to ask questions, and the answers aligned. Edward had taken charge of every part of the funeral. He had insisted on a closed casket. He spoke of his wife's death without emotion. Neighbors said his sorrow seemed practiced, and more than one recalled how carefully he had kept Zona's neck covered.

An order was given to exhume the body. This time a full autopsy was performed, and the doctor was not turned away. Zona's neck was broken. Her windpipe had been crushed. The ligaments at the base of her skull were torn, and deep bruises darkened both sides of her throat. The cause of death was changed to homicide. Edward Shue was arrested for her murder.

At first, the prosecution had no intention of mentioning the ghost. They already had motive, evidence, and witnesses. But the defense believed that letting Mary Jane speak about her dreams would make her look foolish and weaken the case. They were mistaken. She testified without hesitation or sentiment. She told the court what she had seen, why she had gone to the prosecutor, and that without those visits the truth would have remained buried.

The jury listened, not because they were superstitious, but because communication with the dead was not considered unusual in that place or time. It was a shared belief, part of the ordinary landscape of life and loss. Edward Shue was found guilty of first-degree murder and sentenced to life in prison. He died three years later.

Today a historical marker stands near Zona's grave. It tells the story not as legend but as record. The inscription ends with a line that still draws attention: *The only known case in which testimony from a ghost helped convict a murderer.* The state does not file it as myth. And whatever anyone believes about what happened in that house, the part that endures is not the ghost— but the woman who listened, and the court that chose to hear her.

## THE HISTORY

What makes the Greenbrier case unusual isn't only the appearance of a ghost. It's the way that ghost was received. Most spirit tales end quietly with a door closing on its own or a candle flickering without cause. They're told once or twice, then drift into memory. What happened in Greenbrier didn't fade. It advanced. The spirit reached out. The message was plain. And most important of all, someone chose to act on it.

Mary Jane Heaster didn't perform a ritual, at least not in the formal sense. She didn't circle candles or speak in rhyme. What she did was simpler, and closer to the heart of the work. She made space. She lit a lamp, asked a question, and waited. In the language of conjure and ancestor work, that's a valid petition. She may never have used that word, but the form was the same. She sought truth directly from the dead, and when it came, she did not doubt it.

There is a difference between ghost work and spirit work. Ghost work answers what arrives. The dead come uninvited, unsettled, and the worker helps them find rest or meaning. Spirit work begins with intent. It is initiated where the inquirer calls, and the door opens by choice. Mary Jane wasn't haunted; she was informed. That distinction matters. Zona's spirit didn't appear uncertain or symbolic. She gave a full account of how it happened, who was responsible, and what had been done to her.

When the dead speak, it isn't meant to be poetic. In folk practice, messages come from need, not from style. When something must be said, it isn't softened or hidden in signs. The spirit shows what must be seen. That act is all about clarity. The living don't always know how to listen, and the dead have only a brief time to make themselves understood. That mix makes for sharp encounters. When Zona turned her head in her mother's dream, it wasn't a performance. It was anatomy. She showed exactly where the truth had been concealed.

In older cultures, this kind of spirit intervention wasn't treated as a tale. It was treated as evidence. Across rural Europe, when a murder was suspected, the accused was sometimes made to walk past the body. If the corpse bled or shifted, that was taken as proof. In other places, families called directly on the dead, asking them to name whoever had caused the harm. These weren't ornaments of belief but were methods used when law failed or couldn't be trusted. What they share with the Greenbrier case is simple: the dead could still name the truth, and the living were expected to listen.

What Mary Jane did wouldn't have been called magic in her day, but it follows the same order. A question was asked. A response came. Action followed. She sought an answer from the spirit, received it, and carried it to those who could set things right. That pattern of intention, response, and result is the shape of a what we call a spell. The fact that it used no herbs, no charms, and no formal rite doesn't place it outside that definition. The work was done. The spirit answered. And the truth came to light.

In modern terms, the Greenbrier story is an act of ancestral justice. In folk practice, it's common to turn to the dead—especially to family—when the living will not tell the truth. This doesn't call for a séance or ceremony. It often comes through dreams, memory, or signs that repeat until someone pays attention. What matters is how the living respond. When the message is treated as real, it strengthens. The details sharpen, the voice grows steady, and the signs persist until something in the living world begins to shift.

That is what gives the Greenbrier case its weight. The power of the story isn't that a ghost appeared, but that someone believed her. Most would have set the dream aside. Mary Jane did not. She didn't ask the church for approval or wait for neighbors to agree. She took what she was given into a system that hadn't asked for it and refused to let it be dismissed. That act was deliberate, direct, and without ornament. It's what defines the magical heart of the story.

## THE MAGIC & SIGNS

Most ghost stories are quiet. They move in fragments—a sound in the hallway, a face caught in a mirror, a name spoken in a dream. They rarely make themselves easy to tell. They unfold slowly, and by the time the pieces fit together, no one wants to repeat them. That's how they fade. Every so often, though, a story refuses that pattern. The presence doesn't soften. The message doesn't change. And the person who receives it cannot turn away.

One record from Missouri in the late 1800s tells of two sisters. One died without warning. The cause was listed as influenza, but the symptoms didn't fit, and the burial came quick. The surviving sister, Clara, said she began to dream the same dream again and again. Her sister would appear and speak one sentence each time: *Look in the well.* Nothing more. The message never changed.

Weeks later, the town drained its main well for cleaning. At the bottom, they found a sealed glass bottle filled with a fine white powder. It tested as arsenic. No one was charged, but suspicion fell on a man who had been close to the dead woman—and who left town before the year was out. The story stayed. Not because of proof, but because of the dream.

Another account, passed down through family papers from the Appalachian Mountains in the 1930s, tells of a logging accident that the man's mother and widow never accepted. He was said to have fallen from a ridge, his footing uncertain. Those who knew him said otherwise. He was steady, experienced, not the kind to take risks. After the burial, both women said they saw him in the house. Not shadow. Not memory. His boots. His work clothes. The dark bruise along his jaw. He didn't speak. He stood in the hallway, waiting.

The mother, who practiced the old mountain ways, took a lock of his hair and a pair of gloves and buried them beneath a young ash tree. Before she covered the hole, she spoke once: *If you have something to say, speak it to me in my sleep.* That night, the man who had signed the accident report suffered a fatal stroke. Years later, a retired worker quietly admitted that the man had been pushed during a fight and that the company hid the truth to avoid blame. The death certificate was never changed.

Neither of these stories led to a trial. There was no record, no official revision. Yet both are remembered not as ghost tales, but as moments when something refused to stay buried. The lesson isn't that the dead come back for revenge. It's that they come back for recognition. When they're denied that in life, they return to ask it of whoever is still listening.

Stories like these last in families because they carry instruction. They're not told for shock or fear. They explain what happens when a pattern shows itself and the person who sees it refuses to look away—the woman who dreams the same words three nights running, the one who keeps seeing a figure in the hallway no one else believes in, the worker who finds a sealed jar on a trail and chooses to leave it be. These aren't fringe moments. They belong to a larger rhythm of attention. In folk practice, the supernatural isn't rare. It's selective.

## THE WORK

The Greenbrier case is unusual because it ended in a conviction, but it follows a familiar pattern: a death that raises questions, a message that comes by unseen means, and someone willing to carry that message forward without apology. That isn't rare in magic. It isn't rare in death work. What's rare is seeing it carried all the way through.

What endures in the Greenbrier story isn't that a spirit spoke, but that the message was heard and acted on. Most accounts of contact with the dead stop short of change. Someone hears something, feels something, sees something, and then stops there. What happened here was different. The spirit spoke. The living woman heard. And she didn't turn away.

That rhythm of message, reception, and response is the same logic behind any working that asks the dead for truth. This kind of work isn't done for comfort. It isn't about sensing a presence or proving a bond. It's used when something doesn't rest easy, when silence feels wrong, or when an answer is needed that can't come from the living. The purpose isn't to open a door and keep it open. It's to knock, ask clearly, and listen with discipline.

When calling to the dead for clarity, three things matter more than tools or timing: the weight of the question, the willingness to hear the whole answer, and the respect shown once it's done. That balance of intention, reception, and release forms the container. Without it, all a person holds is a feeling. With it, they have an entire magical ritual.

To ask a spirit for truth, begin in a place where you won't be disturbed. It doesn't have to be an altar, but it should be clean, still, and without mirrors. Light a white candle—not for purity, but for visibility. It becomes the focus for your question. Set a glass of spring water or rainwater nearby. Keep something that belongs to the person you're calling. It could be a photograph, a line of handwriting, or a small possession, maybe something that was important to them. Speak the name once, aloud, and ask the question as it stands. No poetry. No ceremony. Only the truth you need to know. Then wait.

There's no set time. Some sit for thirteen minutes. Some until the air shifts. Others until the flame moves or the room itself seems to lean in. However it shows up, if it shows up at all, write it down once the candle is out. Don't speak of it or share it with another. Just keep is private. That's part of the seal. When you're done, pour the water at the base of a tree or leave it at a crossroads. It grounds what was stirred and lets the door close quietly behind it.

This kind of ritual isn't meant for curiosity. It's used when the question already carries weight, and the spirit being asked has reason to care about the answer. It isn't for naming villains or accusing the living. It's for bringing clarity when silence grows too heavy to cross. The reply might come through the candle, through a dream that follows, or through signs that echo the question's tone. The form doesn't matter. What matters is whether the one who asked is ready to hear it.

When the intent moves from receiving truth to

stirring it, when something hidden needs to come forward, the work changes. That spell isn't about connection; it's about motion. It doesn't ask a spirit to speak. It asks a spirit to act. In that case, the materials point the way: a black candle, a name written on brown paper, a nail or iron pin pressed into the wax. Not to bind or harm anyone, but to hold the energy steady. A pinch of graveyard dirt, if you have it, is added not for curse or command, but to call presence. The dirt marks the boundary crossed.

Light the candle with one sentence spoken aloud: *Let what's buried rise*. Then wait. When the candle has burned down, bury the nail and paper near running water or at a crossroads, and leave a coin beside them. The coin isn't payment. It's respect for whatever forces carried the message through. This isn't a punishment spell. It's a revealing spell. It doesn't decide what happens next. It clears the way for truth to stand on its own.

The result is never guaranteed. Spirits don't answer on command. But when the call comes from honest intent and the question is rightfully asked, the silence around the truth begins to loosen. Sometimes it happens quickly. Sometimes it takes months. The spell begins the moment a person speaks the words that no one else will say.

That's what Mary Jane Heaster did. She asked for the truth from someone who could no longer be silenced, and she trusted the answer enough to act on it, even when it cost her comfort or credibility. That's where the real magic lives. Not in the apparition or in the dream, but the act of her following through.

In folk magic, justice rarely arrives with ceremony. It comes through friction, through persistence, through someone who won't let a thing stay buried just because it's easier that way. Whether that happens in a courtroom or in the corner of a kitchen, it matters the same. The dead don't speak without reason. The question is whether the living will listen, and what they'll do once they have.

# The Greenbrier Ghost

In Greenbrier's hills where shadows grow,
A tale still walks from long ago.
A bride was buried, pale and still,
Her mother swore she feels her still.
The house went cold, the silence deep,
But truth won't rest where liars sleep.

The townsfolk said, *it's fainting, dear.*
A proper death—no cause for fear.
But nights turned strange and lamps burned low,
And Zona's mother saw her glow.
She came in dreams, her voice so clear,
"I'll tell you what they hid right here."

Her head bent back, her neck awry,
She showed the mark that would not lie.
She told of rage, of love turned sore,
Of hands that swore to harm no more.
And when the dawn broke, cold and white,
Her mother vowed to set it right.

The lawmen came with doubtful eyes,
They dug the earth and found the guise.
The neck was snapped, the truth was plain—
A ghost had named the hand of pain.
And in that court, before them all,
The dead gave proof, and pride did fall.

They laid her down with prayers once more,
No chains of silence, as before.
The hills grew still, the story spread,
Of how a ghost's words raised the dead.
And every wind that sweeps that glen
Still whispers justice now and then.

So if you walk near sunset's gleam,
And hear a voice between a dream,
Remember, truth has its own breath—
It will not rest in shallow death.
The heart that listens, pure and clear,
May hear her words: *I'm still right here.*

# BURIED IN GLASS: WITCH BOTTLES AND HEXES

It starts the same way in most stories. Someone pulls up a floorboard. Breaks open a wall. Clears out a crawlspace that hasn't seen light in generations. And there it is—a jar. Not modern. Not decorative. Just glass, clouded and sealed with wax gone brittle from age. Inside are the same pieces that turn up again and again: hair, thread, a nail streaked with rust. Sometimes a name. Sometimes a slip of paper too faint to read. The first reaction is rarely surprise. It's recognition—a quiet sense that what they found was meant to stay buried.

What most people call a witch bottle was never meant to be found. In old records, they appear beneath hearthstones in Georgia, behind chimneys in Virginia, and inside the walls of houses across the South and beyond. They weren't forgotten. They were sealed and hidden with purpose. Some were made to protect. Others to bind. A few to break what couldn't be spoken aloud. The names changed—witch bottles, hex jars, trouble jars, but the aim stayed steady: to trap it, to hold it, or to send it back.

In early American homes, the hearth wasn't just for cooking or heat. It was the heart of the house—the center where warmth, work, and prayer all met. Anything placed beneath it became part of the foundation itself. That's why so many of these jars were buried under the fireplace bricks. They were meant to catch what might come down the chimney: illness, envy, or a spirit called by mistake. In British folk tradition, bottles like these often held pins or urine to reflect or confuse a curse. When those customs crossed the Atlantic, the materials changed. Pins became nails. Milk or water became hair or graveyard dirt. The purpose stayed the same, but the language of the spell changed to fit the land.

People who built these bottles understood that power could travel both ways. If the jar was broken before its work was finished, the trouble inside could be released. That's why, when one is uncovered now, the old stories warn against opening it. Even those who say they don't believe in magic will often rebury the jar or move it to the edge of the property rather than throw it away. They may not know the full history, but they still recognize what it stands for—a problem contained, a danger already taken care of. Breaking it feels like undoing someone else's safety net.

Every region has its own version. Along the Carolina coast, bottles sometimes held shells and blue glass beads, charms tied to water spirits and protection from the evil eye. In the mountains, iron nails and red thread were common, chosen for their balance of blood and metal. Farther north, in older cities, jars often held scraps of paper covered in Bible verses. Each variation tells the same story in a different dialect. Protection wasn't symbolic. It was built by hand and hidden in plain sight.

## THE HISTORY

The first known examples trace back to England in the late 1500s, when the word *witch* meant more than suspicion. It meant danger. A neighbor with the wrong look could be blamed for curdled milk, dead livestock, or fever in a house she never entered. When people felt cursed, they didn't go to court. They went to the hearth and built what they could with what they had.

The earliest witch bottles were filled with sharp metal like bent pins, old nails and personal fluids, most often urine, used to link the spell to its maker. These bottles weren't made to bless. They were made to block. Buried upside down near a door or a hearth, they were meant to confuse whatever spirit had been sent. Add hair, spit, or a written name, and the force of the injury could be sent back to its source. It wasn't prayer. It was a countermeasure.

The practice crossed the Atlantic with settlers and enslaved people who carried their own systems beside it. The bottle changed as it traveled. It took new names and found new purposes. By the 1800s in the American South, it had become the trouble jar—a broader tool used not only to defend but to drive, sour, bind, or anchor. The materials shifted with the land. In hoodoo, a jar spell might hold red brick dust, sulfur, graveyard dirt, vinegar, pepper, or broken glass. Always something personal. Always a name. Sometimes a slip of paper, folded and spoken over. Sometimes a body link—hair, nails, a piece of worn cloth. The jar became the vessel for what the worker couldn't say aloud. Once sealed, it spoke for itself.

What mattered most wasn't the bottle but where it

was placed and how it was sealed. Buried under the porch, hidden behind the hearth, or tucked deep inside the walls, these jars weren't meant to be seen. They were built to sit quietly, active and unnoticed, doing their work for as long as needed. Once buried, you didn't speak of it again. You didn't check to see if it was still there. You left it in the dark and trusted it to finish what it had been started to do.

That's why, when people find them now, the reaction is often physical—a change in the air, a tightening in the chest, a quiet pull that feels like warning. Even those who claim not to believe in magic often pause before opening a sealed jar filled with hair and nails. It isn't superstition. It's recognition. Somewhere deeper, they understand this isn't junk. It's a set of instructions. A spell meant to stay active until the job was done or until someone disturbed it.

The idea of sealing harm inside a container and burying it in the foundation of a home doesn't belong to one culture. It appears in layers across continents and centuries because the logic is universal: when danger comes in, you put something in its path. The earliest witch bottles in England were defensive, made to absorb or confuse malevolent forces. But as the practice crossed oceans through colonization, through slavery, or through migration the meaning expanded. In the South, especially within conjure and hoodoo, the jar didn't just guard. It answered.

By the 1800s, trouble jars had become a standard tool across several folk traditions. They could protect, reverse, or press down on a person's path until that person either moved on or changed direction. No initiation was required to make one. What mattered was the material, the belief, and the will to follow through. Red pepper brought heat. Vinegar soured. Rusted nails corroded peace. Graveyard dirt added weight. Thread bound the work together. Blood charged it. And always, there was a name.

The name mattered more than the container. Without it, the jar had no direction. It could hold power but not move it. That's why so many name papers are found inside these jars, even ones sealed a century ago. Sometimes the name is written in full. Sometimes it's a nickname, folded and spoken over. Sometimes it's replaced with hair or a scrap of cloth worn close to the skin. Whatever the form, something in the jar tells it who to hold. Without that link, the jar is only storage, like a sealed battery with no circuit.

Placement carried equal weight. A jar buried under the front steps made the work cling to anyone crossing the threshold. One hidden behind the hearth tied the energy to the heart of the home. Inside a wall, it applied slow, lasting pressure. In Southern practice, jars were sometimes buried beneath bedroom floors to influence intimacy. In court cases, they were set near courthouses to bend testimony. When someone's luck turned or a house felt wrong, the first question a rootworker often asked was simple: *Have you checked under your porch?*

The sealing of them was never symbolic. A wax-sealed jar meant the spell was not meant to be opened, ever. The seal completed the statement. It closed the energy loop. In most cases, the person who built the jar never mentioned it again or left instructions for how it should be handled after their death. These were not performances. They were decisions.

Outside the South, related customs appeared under different names. In Eastern Europe, iron and salt were buried in jars at doorways to block illness. In rural Scotland, bundles of bone and cloth were hidden beneath barn floors to protect livestock. In the Caribbean, people practiced tree burials, driving objects into living trunks to trap harm or slow an enemy's steps. Among the Pennsylvania Dutch, hex jars and bottles were sealed with written prayers and built into the walls. In Creole Catholic homes, a bottle wrapped in cloth might be tucked behind a statue of Mary. It wasn't because the work was hidden from their faith, but because it was woven into it.

Every version of the practice keeps the same shape: danger is near, and a boundary must be drawn. You build a vessel that says *no*. You fill it with materials that carry that message. Then you place it where the line is clearest—where people cross, where air shifts, where energy divides and decides whether to stay or move on. Once set, the jar doesn't need attention. It needs to be left alone.

What historians call ritual debris is often magic that stayed active until someone interfered. That interference, whether it was through curiosity, carelessness, or by accident, releases pressure on something that was sealed for a reason.

## THE MAGIC

When someone finds a sealed jar filled with hair, nails, thread, dirt, or liquid, the first question they ask is what it means. In folk magic, meaning is never a mystery. Every item in a jar is a decision. None of it is filler. The materials speak in the same language as the spell itself—plain, direct, and without metaphor.

Most jars begin with what is called a taglock. In hoodoo, that link is called a personal concern. Hair is the most common, but nail clippings, saliva, or cloth worn against the body serve the same purpose. They give the work direction. A jar without a taglock still holds power, but it drifts. It becomes a signal with no target. When a name appears, especially one written on paper that's been folded or spoken over, the link turns from symbol to instruction.

Thread appears often, usually black or red. Black thread closes a situation. Red keeps it in motion. The thread may be knotted, looped, or wrapped around other objects inside the jar. That act isn't decoration.

It builds entanglement. When the thread binds a pin or a nail, the spell turns active. It's made to restrict, to harm, or to trap. Each knot seals a spoken intention, even if the words were never written down. The thread carries that intention into the heart of the jar.

Rust is rarely coincidence. Rusted nails and pins mark slow damage—the kind that creeps instead of cuts. Clean iron can block, but rusted iron seeps. It changes what it touches. That's why old nails are used in jar spells meant to wear something down over time. A new nail cuts. A rusted one rots.

Graveyard dirt changes a jar completely. It adds weight and summons presence. It can call on the authority of the dead, the silence of judgment, or the finality of closure. Where the dirt is gathered determines its tone. From a stranger's grave, it applies neutral pressure. From a family grave, it carries protection. From the grave of a killer or a wronged soul, it calls retribution. The worker decides what kind of dirt the jar requires and where it should rest.

Heat ingredients act as fuel. Red pepper keeps the jar alive and agitated. Vinegar sours peace. Sulfur deepens severity. None of these are chosen for symbolism—they're chosen for what they do. Red pepper bites. Sulfur lingers. Vinegar burns and eats through what it touches. These elements make sure the spell doesn't go to sleep. As long as the contents stay moist and the seal holds, the power keeps moving.

Some jars hold liquid—urine, alcohol, vinegar, or oil. The liquid carries the other materials and keeps them from drying out. A dry jar binds or restricts. A wet jar flows, influences, or spreads. In protection work, saltwater cleanses and contains. In harsher work, urine ties the jar to its source and sets the working in motion. Whatever the liquid, its purpose is the same: it moves.

The seal defines the jar's state. A wax seal means the work is closed, complete, and final. In most cases, a wax-sealed jar isn't meant to be opened, not even by the one who made it. A screw-top or corked jar, by contrast, is temporary. It can be reopened, fed, or burned. When wax is poured across the lid or mouth of the jar, that act draws the boundary. It says the spell is finished and should not be touched again.

Placement decides how the jar behaves. One buried beneath the front steps affects everyone who crosses the threshold. One under a bed works on what's personal. One behind a hearth influences the whole house. A jar kept near heat stays active. One buried in the cold holds steady until disturbed. Each position reinforces the spell's purpose. The jar becomes part of the structure like a quiet instruction sealed inside the bones of a home.

If a jar like this is found and broken, especially by someone who doesn't understand what it was built to do, the effect is rarely positive. A spell sealed in glass can stay active for decades without notice. The moment it cracks, the seal opens and the pressure releases. Whoever breaks it takes on what it was meant to contain.

That's why traditional workers warn against opening a jar until its purpose is known, and never unless you're ready to carry what comes out.

## THE SIGNS

Most of these jars sit unnoticed for years. They stay sealed, undisturbed, remembered only by the person who made them. As long as the container holds, the work stays where it was set. When a jar is opened by accident, curiosity, or intent, something in the air changes. The reaction isn't always immediate, but it's rarely neutral.

People who have found them describe the same pattern over and over again. First, the room changes. Not in temperature, but in weight. The air grows heavier. Pets act differently. The sound inside the house sharpens or goes flat. Then come the disruptions, small at first. Electronics misfire. Lights flicker without reason. Sleep turns uneven. Dreams repeat. Some people develop headaches. Others say the house becomes hard to stay in—not dangerous, just uneasy.

In East Tennessee, a family renovating a farmhouse

found a jar sealed inside the wall behind their living-room chimney. It held hair, black thread, bent nails, and a square of paper with a name they didn't recognize. The wax was intact. When the jar was pulled free, the atmosphere in the house changed. Footsteps moved along the baseboards at night. A door that had stayed shut for years began to drift open even when latched. After three weeks, the family wrapped the jar in cloth, buried it at a crossroads, and poured whiskey over the site. The disturbances stopped.

In another case, a contractor in Mississippi dislodged a mason jar from behind the tile of an old bathroom wall. It fell and broke. Inside were a clump of hair, a nail, and part of a playing card—the queen of spades. In the days that followed, both homeowners reported nausea, restless sleep, and strange electrical issues with devices that had always worked. A local worker advised them to gather the pieces, cleanse the space with Florida Water, and bury the remains in neutral ground with a coin and a pinch of salt. Within a week, the house settled.

These aren't stories of horror. They're stories of imbalance. The jar was made to hold something. When that containment breaks, the pressure has nowhere to go. Even when the spell was meant for protection, its sudden release can still stir the air. The same way opening a sealed letter sends its message into motion, breaking a jar releases the instruction sealed inside.

Not every jar causes disturbance when found. If the materials have faded, the seal has failed, or the liquid has long since evaporated, the spell may have gone inert. But if the contents are intact, if the taglock is still present and the power was never dismissed, the work remains active. It doesn't need the original maker to complete its circuit. It only needs recognition.

That's why traditional workers handle jar disposal with care. A spell sealed in glass isn't leftover magic. It's a contract. When you open it, you become the last person to touch the intention. The spell doesn't care whether you meant to join it. It only knows that the line has been reopened.

The solution isn't panic. It's respect. You don't keep the jar as a souvenir. You don't study it like a record. You don't bring it inside to cleanse or display. You close it, ground it, and return it to neutral space. Leave a small offering in acknowledgment, even if you don't know its history. That isn't superstition. It's maintenance.

In folk practice, the rule is simple: when you disturb something that was sealed with intention, you finish the handling with intention. If you don't, the imbalance finds its own way to close. It may show up as restless sleep, as silence where there used to be ease, or as a spell beginning to move again without knowing who it's meant for.

The point isn't to fear the jar. It's to understand that anything sealed and buried was never meant to be idle. It keeps its work until someone tells it to stop.

## THE WORK

A sealed jar is one of the simplest ways to mark where the line stands. It doesn't shout. It doesn't glow. But it holds. It can hold on for years, even decades, without reinforcement as long as the container stays closed and the space around it remains undisturbed. That kind of magic lasts because it was never built to impress. It was made to protect, to bind, to interrupt, or to remind what's unseen that it has been noticed and answered.

Two kinds of work grow from this system: the jar you build with intention, and the jar you find that was never meant to be yours.

When you need to set a boundary, it may be between you and someone who keeps disturbing your peace. It can also be between your home and energy that refuses to leave. A protection jar is the easiest place to start. You do not need rare herbs or old bottles. Use a container with a tight lid, materials that feel solid, and stay focused while you work in silence.

Start with a petition, not a wish. Write what you want the jar to hold back. Use plain paper and cross it with a phrase that names the work: peace, protection, boundary. Fold the paper inward three times toward yourself. This isn't a spell of release. It's reinforcement.

Place the petition at the bottom of the jar. Add a layer of black salt or crushed eggshell, something that absorbs and neutralizes. Wind red thread around a bent nail, tight and deliberate, and set it on top. Add an herb with structure: rosemary for clarity and sealing, bay for strength. Finish with a shard of mirror or a piece of broken glass turned outward. That tells the energy to reflect what doesn't belong.

Seal the jar with a tight lid. Heat a black candle and drip wax around the rim until no part of the thread or paper is visible. As you work, speak once and with weight: *What's mine stays mine. What's not gets cut. This jar holds the line.*

Then bury it. For home protection, place it beneath the front porch or beside a gate. For personal protection, bury it near the place you return to most often. Don't feed it. Don't check on it. The power lives in the sealing, not the watching.

If you uncover a jar that you didn't make or request, the handling changes, especially if it's broken, leaking, or unsealed. Start with containment. Don't touch the contents directly. Wrap the jar first in black cloth, then in foil to keep the power from spreading. Clean the area where it was found with something sharp-scented: Florida Water, vinegar, or camphor. Speak clearly as you wipe the space: *This spell is done. This charge is closed. What was held is now released.* Then cleanse yourself with saltwater, smoke, or any method your practice uses to steady the line between one power and the next.

Carry the wrapped jar off your property. Don't rush the burial, but don't delay it either. A graveyard is best. A crossroads will do. The edge of a wooded space is enough. Bury it fully. Don't speak over the site. Don't look back. If it feels right, leave a coin or a piece of candy as a marker—not as thanks, but as acknowledgment. You're closing someone else's work, and that act deserves to be noted.

This isn't about fear. It's about clearing interference so your home can return to being a home, not a vessel for magic that was never yours.

It doesn't matter whether the jar was made a century ago or last week. What matters is that it was sealed with intention. If you're the one who broke that seal, even by accident, you're responsible for what follows. Folk magic has always made that part plain: a spell remembers the hand that finishes it.

# DEATH KNOCKS – THE COFFIN WAS SCREAMING

In some Appalachian houses, silence is just silence. In others, it means something. The air stops moving but isn't soothing. The hallway refuses to warm no matter how many times you check the stove. The sound in the next room shifts just enough for you to notice, but not enough to figure out what it was. In those houses, death doesn't come quietly. It gives signs. And once you've lived in a place like that, you stop mistaking them for anything else.

The most common is the knock. Always three. Never loud. It doesn't strike with force. It lands with timing. Some say it comes from the front door. Others swear it's inside the walls. A few say it sounds like it's just behind the headboard of the bed. Whatever the version, the rule stays the same: when it comes, someone is already marked. Families who've lived in the same house for generations can name who heard it last time and who was gone the next week. No one explains it. They just say, *I heard it,* and everyone knows what that means.

These signs don't depend on belief in ghosts. Most people who speak of them never use that word at all. What they describe is pattern. When the same sound comes before three deaths in a row, you start listening for it. When the same picture falls from the wall every time someone gets sick, you stop hanging it back up. In those houses, superstition isn't a show or a ritual. It's common knowledge.

The knock is only one of many signs. In some homes its wings instead like a slow, heavy fluttering around the eaves. Too heavy for birds. Too steady for bats. People call it the death bird. When it circles three times without making a sound, the meaning is clear: someone in the house has already been counted.

Pictures falling, candles going cold, clocks stopping for no reason—each carries weight in households that keep the old ways. When a photograph drops from the wall without being touched, especially one showing someone still living, the room goes quiet. When the flame on the hearth bends low and refuses to rise no matter how dry the wood, the silence around it thickens. It doesn't have to be dramatic. The change is enough to make you notice.

In these houses, death isn't a shock. It's a shift. The rhythm of the home slows. People sweep the porch again even if it's clean. The good blanket is folded at the foot of the bed. Mirrors are covered without a word. Not because someone has died, but because something in the house says it's time to prepare.

## THE HISTORY

The covering of mirrors is one of the oldest and most steady death customs in the Appalachian region. It's also one of the least explained. Nobody pauses to say why. They just reach for a towel. In rooms where someone is dying, reflective surfaces are treated as risks. Not because they're portals in the storybook sense, but because they might catch a spirit in passing. A soul that sees its reflection before it's gone might hesitate. It might mistake the image for what it left behind and stay too long. So, the mirrors are covered.

Not to stop death, but to give it a clear exit.

The same logic extends to clocks. When someone dies, the clock is stopped. Not only to mark the moment, but to divide time—before and after, breath and silence. Some families leave it still for three days. Some wait until the funeral ends. Others wait until the last visitor has gone. The message stays the same: time doesn't move forward in this house until the spirit has gone with it.

And sometimes the clocks are the first to act. They stop without a reason or turn backward once—just enough to catch your eye if you happen to be looking. Someone always is. Later, they'll say, "It started running the wrong way," like they still can't explain it. They didn't mention it before the burial. Thought it was just them. But it never is. Signs don't ask to be believed. They just happen, and you know what they mean.

## THE MAGIC

Some signs are felt more than seen. A room turns cold without reason. A window refuses to stay shut. A chair shifts slightly out of place. None of this means much to people who don't live in the house, but to those who have watched the pattern for years, these moments aren't random. They're markers. Something is moving through.

In older stories, there's mention of a sound like a

coffin being built. Not hammering exactly, more the slow creak of wood under weight, as if a box were being dragged across a floor no one is standing on. In families where someone had been a carpenter, the sound was said to have its own rhythm. They called it the setting of lid nails. Not driven. Just set.

None of this is spoken of as ghost lore. It isn't about the soul returning. It's about the house taking notice. The signs don't follow belief. They follow routine. If you were raised in a place like that, no one has to tell you when to cover the mirror or open a window. You do it because someone else did before you.

That's how death moves in a house that pays attention. Not with sirens or a flashy announcement. With knocks. With silence. With a small shift in the air that reminds someone to check the locks, draw the shade, and leave one window open just in case.

Most death customs among mountain people aren't called magic by the ones who keep them. They're simply what's done. But when you look at the pattern such as the timing, the order, and the events, it's easy to see the structure. These are forms of magical work. Quiet ones. Built from repetition and need. They don't use ritual tools. They use what's already part of the house: doorframes, mirrors, clocks, and flame.

Take the clocks. Stopping them isn't a sentimental act. It's a boundary. In folk systems, time isn't only a measure of hours; it's a container. If it keeps running after someone dies, it can blur the line between presence and absence. Spirits move through rhythm, and if that rhythm isn't paused, they may not recognize that they've gone.

That's why some families stop the clock the moment death comes. Others wait until the house settles and they know the soul has departed.

Covering mirrors follows the same logic. Across Appalachian, Southern, Caribbean, and Eastern European traditions, mirrors are believed to catch what shouldn't linger. It isn't superstition. It's recognition of what reflection does. A mirror doubles things, echoes them back, and sometimes holds onto them if you're not careful.

If a spirit sees itself in the glass before it's fully gone, it can lose direction. It might stay. You don't risk that. You don't explain it. You just cover the mirror. Whatever's close at hand will do whether it's a towel, a shirt, a handkerchief. The material isn't what matters. It's the interruption. Breaking the reflection keeps the spirit moving.

In some homes, glass picture frames are covered as well, especially portraits, especially faces. If the dead feel drawn back toward the living, the last thing you want is for them to see their own image and mistake it for a place to rest. The reasoning isn't symbolic. It's practical. Keep the path clear. Don't give the spirit a reason to linger.

## THE SIGNS

In western North Carolina, a white farmhouse sits on the edge of a ridge that's been held by the same family for four generations. No one there calls themselves superstitious. No one talks about ghosts. But when death nears, the knocks come. Always in the same place, on the wall between the hallway and the parlor. Always after midnight. Always followed by silence. Not the quiet of rest, but the kind that settles over a room like fog. Once the knocks sound, no one speaks of it. The next morning they start making calls. Nobody has ever died in that hallway, but that's where the sound lives, and that's enough.

In parts of eastern Kentucky, people still say, *If the fire goes out while the wood's still good, someone's being made ready.* That's the phrase—*made ready.* Not taken. Not cursed. Just moved into position. A woman from Letcher County told a story about her uncle's dog that howled at a wall for an hour one night—not at the door, not the window, but a bare stretch of wall. The next morning they learned her cousin's youngest had died in another town. Pneumonia. Sudden. No warning. The uncle had been carving a toy for that child the day before and left it half-finished on the porch. Nobody ever touched it again.

Most of these stories don't come from people who claim to practice magic. They come from people who've seen the same pattern repeat more times than they can explain away. They'll tell you the knock might have been plumbing. The creak could have been the wind. The scent of tobacco in the bedroom after the funeral was probably just a draft. But they pause when they say it. And if you ask them again, maybe after the next funeral, they'll tell you what they left out the first time. That it felt different. That it felt true.

That's the shape of this kind of knowing. It doesn't arrive with certainty. It arrives in a moment—a silence that makes you check the hallway, a clock that stops for no reason, a fire that leans forward just enough to feel seen. And sometimes it doesn't happen in the house where death will come. Sometimes it happens next door. Sometimes three counties away. These signs don't follow fences. They follow connection.

The knock might land where someone is still alive but already counted. A mirror might fog in a house the dead never visited but where someone still dreams of them. A dog might growl at the base of a tree, not because anything is buried there, but because the ground remembers grief and waits for the next one.

These signs aren't always warnings. Sometimes they're acknowledgments. The house doesn't just hold the living. It makes room for what comes next. The signs tell the people inside that the time for asking is over. That now is the time for salt at the door, a candle by the window, and a bowl of water set down quietly in a room that feels heavier than it should.

The people who notice these things don't ask for them. They carry the knowledge with them. Usually without acknowledgment, sometimes without choice. They're the ones who open a window without being told. The ones who feel a change in the air before the phone rings. The ones who know what to do when a clock suddenly runs backward, even if they never say it aloud. Not everyone in a family senses it, but there's almost always one who does.

And when that person tells the story later, they won't claim certainty. They'll just say, *It was strange timing.* That's how you know the old work is still being done, even when no one calls it magic.

## THE WORK

When death comes close, most people want peace. Not a guarantee. Not a delay. Just peace. For the one leaving and for those who remain. That's what these signs and gestures have always been about—not control, but containment. When the air shifts, you meet it. When the knock comes, you listen. You don't try to change what's already moving. You clear the way.

When death is near, the house changes. Time folds. Rooms feel layered. People speak less. The work that follows is simple, structured, and quiet. You're not there to redirect fate. You're there to support the passage and to keep anything from lingering that wasn't meant to stay.

The first spell is one used in Appalachian and Southern households alike, often by people who wouldn't use that word but still passed it down as necessary knowledge. It begins with a clean cloth laid over every mirror in the room where the death is expected. The mirror is covered not out of fear, but to prevent confusion. The spirit doesn't need to see itself in the crossing. That belief doesn't require explanation. It's lasted because it continues to serve.

Next, a white candle is set near a window. Not centered. Not ceremonial. Just steady. It burns through the waiting hours to hold light in the space and to offer a point of orientation for what can't be seen. In rooms where a window can be opened safely, one pane is lifted after the final breath—not to invite something in, but to let what's leaving pass out cleanly. The window stays open until the candle burns out or until the room settles. The closing is done without comment.

At the foot of the bed, place a bowl of water. Nothing added. No herbs. Just clean water in a plain vessel. It draws stray power away from the living and gives the spirit a place to settle if the passing is slow or uncertain. If no one is present when death occurs, the water still holds. It's poured out the next morning—

ideally at a crossroads, though any place off the main property will do. The bowl is washed, put away, and never used again for guests or children. That, too, is part of the spell.

In some homes, a black thread is tied with three knots and laid along the windowsill. One knot for departure. One for the line between the worlds. One to keep the living from carrying what isn't theirs. When the thread is removed it's usually buried at the edge of the property. That closes the circuit. You don't keep the thread and you don't burn it because it isn't banishment. It's a boundary.

This work doesn't end grief or take away loss. It just helps the house remember its purpose after the spirit has gone.

If, in the days or weeks that follow, the room still feels unsettled—if the air won't move, or sleep won't come, or something about the space feels heavier than sorrow then you know the work isn't done. The next spell is for clearing what remains. It's not about force. It's about release.

Begin by boiling rosemary or pine needles. If you can't boil them, burn them carefully and carry the smoke through every room that feels thick or weighted. The scent should rise and move. If it lingers low, keep going. When the air smells like something both fresh and ancient, like weather through an open window, move to the next step.

Mix vinegar and water and use it to wipe down window frames, doorways, handles, and corners that don't get touched often. The goal isn't cleanliness. It's movement. As you clean, speak softly—not prayer, not performance—just steady words: *This space returns to the living. What has left may keep moving. What remains may rest.*

If you have a small piece of iron—an old key, a nail, a rusted screw—place it in a bowl of water and leave it in the quietest room overnight. It pulls down the charge. It grounds what hasn't been named. In the morning, pour the water off the property. The base of a tree works. A river works better. A crossroads works best. You don't explain what you're doing. You just do it. That's the part people forget. Death work doesn't ask for belief. It asks for completion.

When it's done right, the house feels different. Not lighter, exactly. More like it has been corrected. The mirrors can be uncovered. The clock restarted. The candle put away until next time. And there will be a next time. Because this isn't work you do once. It's work you remember how to do when it matters.

# SHARP MAGIC – RITUAL KNIVES AND NAILS

You don't find a blade under the porch or a nail behind the chimney by accident. Not in folk magic. Not in the South. And not when it's wrapped in thread, marked with a name, or set in dirt just deep enough for time to cover it without erasing it. These aren't objects. They're decisions. They were placed with purpose, and if you don't know what that purpose was, it's better to leave them where they are.

In Southern conjure, Appalachian rootwork, and in quiet corners of magic around the world, sharp objects fix energy, cut ties, set boundaries, and send messages that don't need to be spoken. A knife buries intent. A nail pins it in place. When either one is hidden—wrapped in red thread, sealed in wax, or buried under a step where people cross without thinking—it isn't decoration. It's protection. It keeps something where it belongs or stops what shouldn't return from crossing the line again.

Knives in folk magic aren't ceremonial. They're not polished or displayed. They're tools. A black-handled blade clears spiritual residue, draws lines across thresholds, and cuts emotional cords that won't break on their own. The blade is drawn through the air just above the skin—not to wound, but to separate. In Appalachian homes, knives were slipped under pillows to block nightmares or stop the spirit pressure called witch riding. Under beds, they broke the hold of bad dreams. Buried under doorframes, they warned off whatever might try to come through uninvited. Each action had purpose. None of it was ornament. It worked because it was done right, not because it looked like magic.

Once a blade has been used in this way, it carries memory. That's why working knives aren't repurposed. You don't cut vegetables with the same knife you use to uncross a client. You don't open mail with the blade that's drawn spiritual boundaries. Once it's been charged for magic, it remains a tool for that purpose alone. Anything else blurs the line. Anything else risks carrying that energy where it doesn't belong.

## THE HISTORY

Nails hold a different place in the work. Iron has always been a metal of weight. Long before it became common, it was treated as protection—dense, unyielding, elemental. In the British Isles, iron was nailed into doors to keep witches out. Horseshoes hung over thresholds, open side up to catch good fortune or open side down to pour protection over whoever passed beneath. Across Africa and throughout its diasporas, iron is sacred to spirits of fire and war, Ogoun among them. That belief crossed the Atlantic and settled deep in the American South.

Nails became part of the hoodoo and conjure toolkit not as props, but as instruments. Rusted nails in jars sour conditions slowly. Fresh nails anchor protection. In graveyard work, nails pulled from old coffins, or forged to resemble them, lock energy in place and mark what should not be disturbed. They appear in footstep magic as well, driven through paper or namework and nailed into thresholds, shoes, or fences to bind movement, slow progress, or weigh a person down until the spell is released.

Railroad spikes are the same idea on a larger scale. They anchor property lines, fix spiritual grids, and keep unwanted energy from seeping through the corners of a space. They aren't buried shallow. They're driven deep—one at each corner of a lot or along an old travel path.

The use of blades and nails isn't limited to the South. In Slavic practice, iron was laid beside a newborn to prevent spirit interference. In Scotland, a knife kept near the cradle was said to block fairy theft. In Creole Catholic homes, knives were placed near the foot of the bed for new mothers and under pillows for the dying—not for harm, but to mark the boundary between this world and the next. The same principle appears in Haitian Vodou, where iron stands for protection, strength, and resolve, especially in the presence of warrior spirits.

The work is consistent across regions. A knife cuts what must be cut. A nail holds what shouldn't move. When they're buried, wrapped, or rusted, they aren't trash. They're active.

If you find one and it isn't yours, the question isn't what it is. It's what it was doing. If it was guarding a boundary, it may still be guarding. If it was holding something down, it may be the only thing keeping that energy in place. Pull it up without knowing, and you may reopen what someone else already closed.

There's no passive use for a blade in folk magic. A knife doesn't hold neutral energy. It holds memory. Once it has been used to cut a cord, seal a boundary, or clear off spiritual residue, it doesn't go back to being an ordinary knife. From that point on, it becomes a tool of magical work, and you have to treat it that way.

## THE MAGIC

The first rule of using a magical blade is separation. You don't use your working knife to slice vegetables, open packages, or clean under your nails. You don't keep it in a kitchen drawer. The edge isn't what makes it powerful—it's the action. The knife holds charge from what it has been used for. A blade that was used for reversal work keeps that charge. A blade that was used for healing keeps that, too. You don't mix those purposes. You don't confuse the tool.

Cord-cutting is one of the clearest examples of this kind of work. A red thread that carries the emotional or spiritual tie you want to release is cut in one clean stroke. No hesitation. No sawing. You speak the person's name or the name of the pattern—the addiction, the betrayal, the habit that refuses to let go, and then you cut. Afterward, the thread is burned or buried, and the knife is cleaned in salt, smoke, or sunlight, depending on your system. This isn't because the knife is dirty. It's because it is still holding the energy of the break, and that energy needs a place to go. Otherwise, it stays in the room.

Another form of this work is called sweeping. That is when a knife is passed just above a person's skin, starting from the top of the head and moving all the way down to the soles of the feet with the edge facing outward. But it never touches the skin—it hovers just above it. Sweeping is more about spiritual maintenance than ceremony. The blade is meant to clear or cut away whatever is clinging to you. So, the knife isn't the doctor in this situation. It is the scalpel that removes any festering magic.

For homes and thresholds, a knife can be placed under the bed with the edge facing out to guard against spiritual interference during sleep. It can also be buried beneath a front step or driven into a doorframe, blade down, to make the message clear: this boundary is closed. Spirits understand that kind of language. Energy that doesn't belong won't cross unless it's been invited.

Nails work under a different kind of logic. A nail is a holding tool. In magical work, it fixes energy in place. When someone writes a name on paper, folds it away from themselves, and drives a nail through it, they've anchored that name to the condition. In jars, nails keep a souring or protective spell from unraveling. In land work, they hold the corners steady. The nails make the invisible line visible to whatever might try to cross it.

Rust adds another layer of intention. Rusted nails don't just hold—they corrode. They grind. They're used when something needs to decay: a relationship, a falsehood, a rival's luck. That's why coffin nails, whether real or symbolic, are used in heavier baneful work. It isn't about the grave. It's about the nature of rust which is slow, heavy, and deliberate.

When nails are used for movement-binding, they're often driven into worn shoes, wooden floorboards, or carved doll forms. These aren't curse theatrics. They're precision spells. The nail pins the energy down. The placement decides the direction. If a nail is hammered through a name paper and hidden in a tree or fencepost, the goal is to fix that person's influence and to keep it in one place so it can't move.

And like blades, nails remember. If you dig one up by accident and don't know why it was set, you don't keep it. You treat it like a spell caught mid-sentence. Because that's exactly what it is.

There's an old saying in conjure: *Don't pull up what you didn't bury.* Most people only need to hear that once—usually after they've already ignored it.

## THE SIGNS

Stories like this show up all over the South. Someone tears up a floorboard, patches a wall, or digs near a porch post and finds something sharp where nothing should be. A knife wrapped in flannel, rusted dark. A nail hammered into a beam, red thread still clinging to its head. Some think it's trash and throw it away. Others clean it up and hang it as decoration. That's when things begin to turn.

In north Georgia, a couple renovating an old farmhouse found a knife behind the fireplace bricks. It was wrapped in fabric, tied off, and tucked neatly behind the masonry. They thought it looked rustic and set it on a shelf. Within a week, their dog wouldn't go near the hearth. Lights in the front room flickered, even after an electrician checked the wiring. Both started having the same dream on the same night, same image of standing in a field, holding something they couldn't let go of.

A local rootworker told them the knife had been set for boundary protection. The fireplace is the center of a home, and that blade had been guarding it for decades. When they pulled it free, they opened the center line and threw the house off balance.

They buried the knife under a cedar tree with salt and cloth, spoke the name of the house aloud, and left whiskey at the roots. The flickering stopped. The dog settled down. And three months later, driving down a road they'd never taken before, they passed a field that looked exactly like the one from their dreams. Same fence. Same slope. No reason for it. Just recognition.

In east Tennessee, another story tells of a boy's shoe that kept disappearing—always the left one. It turned up outside three mornings in a row. His parents laughed it off until they found it nailed to the porch rail with a bent iron spike. Beneath it was a folded name paper. Not the boy's name, but his mother's. Written in pencil. Her maiden name.

That wasn't a prank. It was a spell. A slow movement-binding, the kind that wears someone down before they realize they've been held in place. They burned the paper, salted the porch, and took down the rail post completely. Whatever it was, it stopped. But they never learned who left it, and no one in the neighborhood claimed to know what it meant.

In Mississippi, a man insulating the crawl space under his house found a black-handled knife embedded in the dirt. It was wrapped in hair. No note. No cloth. Just waiting. He hadn't been sleeping well for months. His brother had stopped speaking to him after an argument that made no sense. He found the knife while crawling under the back steps. He didn't touch it. Just looked. That night, the dreams returned stronger than before—same person, same argument, same phrase repeating: *Say it again.*

Hair is personal-link magic. When it's joined to a blade, it's either release or restraint. The placement told the rest of the story—buried under the threshold, the place where tension entered and never left.

He removed the knife carefully and reburied it across town near a stream. With it, he left a written release: *This energy is done. This house is closed.* He cut ties with his brother for good, cleansed the house, and said the place finally exhaled after two years of holding its breath.

These aren't horror stories. There's no jump scare. Only the kind of pressure that builds when a tool made for boundary or release is interrupted midwork. These tools weren't decorative. They were made to act. And they don't stop acting until someone closes them out correctly.

That's why when you find a nail where no nail should be, or a knife sitting where no knife belongs, you don't treat it like junk. You don't clean it. You don't hang it like art. You stop. You feel. You ask what it might be holding. And you remember the rule that came before the rest: don't touch what you didn't bury, unless you're ready to face what it's still holding down.

Every culture with a living folk tradition agrees on one thing about tools that cut or pierce: once they've been set to work, they no longer belong to ordinary life. You can bless with them. You can banish with them. But you never handle them without intention. Sharp tools are language made physical. They say what you mean to say, whether you think about the words or not.

Knives and nails define the edge between blessing and harm. That edge isn't moral. It's mechanical. A blade doesn't care if it frees or wounds—it only knows that something has been divided. A nail doesn't decide whether it's anchoring protection or fastening a curse—it only knows how to hold. That's why this kind of work demands clarity before anything else. You have to know what you're cutting, what you're fixing, and what will follow once the act is done. Because once the steel moves, you can't pull the intent back out of it.

## THE WORK

When the goal is protection, the work starts at the corners. In old conjure and Appalachian practice, the simplest way to seal a space is with four nails (iron, never steel) driven into the boundaries of the home. Each nail marks a point of containment. Before they're set, they're cleaned with saltwater or rubbed with Florida Water to clear away any energy that isn't yours. Then you walk the property line in silence. Move clockwise if you're holding peace in. Move counterclockwise if you're sending something out. At each corner, drive the nail deep, speak your claim once—no script, just words that feel true, and sprinkle a pinch of black salt or crushed eggshell over the head before moving on. When you return to where you started, the line is closed. You don't announce it. You don't decorate it. You go inside and let the house settle.

The same idea applies in smaller spaces. In an apartment, a single nail behind the doorframe works. A piece of iron under a windowsill. A spike laid flat beneath a welcome mat. The power is in the placement, not the display. When the work is right, you'll feel it. There will be a quietness in the air, a stillness that wasn't there before. That's the sign the house recognizes the boundary again.

When the goal is release, the blade takes over. The cleanest cord-cutting isn't dramatic. It's deliberate. A thread or cord is tied to represent what binds you: a relationship, a resentment, a habit that keeps circling back. Hold the thread tight, light a candle, and draw your working knife across it in one smooth stroke. Speak the intention as you cut: *This tie is ended. What was shared is finished.* Dispose of the pieces. Some burn them. Others bury them. Either way, they aren't kept. Wipe the knife with salt or smoke and put it away. You don't use it for anything ordinary afterward. It has said its piece.

In both kinds of work, the key is finality. The iron nail must be driven until it doesn't move. The blade must cut all the way through. Hesitation weakens the boundary and leaves the spell half-alive, which is how things start to echo. Folk magic doesn't forgive half measures.

When you're finished, close the act aloud. Even a single sentence is enough: *This work is finished.* Spoken closure seals what the metal has already done in form. Without it, the tool keeps listening for commands. That's how restless energy lingers.

The rest is maintenance. Check your corners after storms, after hard arguments, or after long visits from people who leave the space feeling drained. If a nail loosens, drive it back in. If a knife used for cutting feels heavy or dull, wash it in saltwater and leave it under moonlight. Sharp magic likes to stay sharp. It's not sentiment. It's upkeep.

These spells may look simple, but they hold one of the oldest truths in folk practice: protection and banishment are the same motion turned in different directions. You drive the nail or you pull it. You cut toward yourself or away. You choose which. And once you choose, the tool carries that order until someone changes it.

So before you pick up the rusted nail beneath your porch or the black-handled knife behind your door, stop and ask the first question every worker learns: *What line was this meant to hold?* If you can answer that, you already know what to do next. If you can't, leave it buried.

In both kinds of work, the key is finality. The iron nail must be driven until it doesn't move. The blade must cut all the way through. Hesitation weakens the boundary and leaves the spell half-alive, which is how things start to echo.

When you're finished, close the act aloud. Even a single sentence is enough: *This work is finished.* Spoken closure seals what the metal has already done in form. Without it, the tool keeps listening for commands. That's how restless energy lingers.

The rest is maintenance. Check your corners after storms, after hard arguments, or after long visits from people who leave the space feeling drained. If a nail loosens, drive it back in. If a knife used for cutting feels heavy or dull, wash it in saltwater and leave it under moonlight.

These spells may look simple, but they hold one of the oldest truths in folk practice: protection and banishment are the same motion turned in different directions. You drive the nail or you pull it. You cut toward yourself or away. You choose which. And once you choose, the tool carries that order until someone changes it.

So before you pick up the rusted nail beneath your porch or the black-handled knife behind your door, stop and ask the first question every worker learns: *What line was this meant to hold?* If you can answer that, you already know what to do next. If you can't, leave it buried. Sharp magic remembers its orders long after everyone else forgets.

# OMENS IN THE OVEN

Your grandmother didn't need a spellbook to know when something was off. She didn't need to read cards or check charts or ask the neighbor what they thought. She paid attention to what fell on the floor, to which burner hissed for no reason, to how the dough moved when it was supposed to rise but didn't. She dropped a fork, looked over her shoulder, and said, "Company's coming." And nine times out of then, they showed up.

In homes where people lived by what they could cook, preserve, and stretch, the kitchen wasn't a cozy symbol of home. It was the place where the spiritual and the practical shared the same shelf. No robes. No incense. Just heat, instinct, and whatever tools were within reach. That was enough. If the bread split down the center, if the milk soured after sundown, if the salt disappeared from where it had just been set, that meant something. And the people who could read those changes didn't call it magic. They called it paying attention.

The hearth has always carried weight. Long before kitchens became rooms with backsplashes and barstools, the fire was where protection lived. In ancient Rome, offerings were fed to the goddess Vesta through flame usually with items like flour, oil, or salt to keep the household in balance. If that fire went out, it was a bad sign for everyone under the roof. In Slavic homes, the *domovoi*—the house spirit— was said to live behind the stove. Feed him well and keep his space clean, and the livestock stayed healthy, the pots boiled well, and the bread rose right. Neglect him, and spoons cracked, food spoiled, and sickness followed. Those things weren't superstition. That was just how life worked.

## THE HISTORY

In African traditions carried to the Americas through enslavement, the kitchen stayed sacred—not in title, but in function. Spices weren't just for flavor. They carried purpose: heat, defense, clarity. Salt by the door. Simmer pots that eased fevers and softened tempers. Garlic hung where trouble tried to enter. Pepper added to food when a lie needed burning out. Those workings weren't written down. They were passed along while stirring greens or teaching how to keep a pot from boiling over when someone's energy was too much to handle.

The goal was never to decorate the house with magic. It was to keep the house standing.

In Jewish kitchens, the lighting of Shabbat candles marked the line between sacred and ordinary time— and also between safety and vulnerability. That small flame did more than honor tradition. It guarded the household. In rural European homes, the midwife and the healer often worked at the same stove. They read the same pantry. If the biscuits failed, if the fire died overnight, if the eggs cracked too clean or refused to crack at all, they understood the message.

They were signs, and they appeared in ordinary ways: a dropped utensil, burned bread, crooked bubbles in a pot that should have boiled smooth. You didn't have to study to see them. You just had to be someone who paid attention.

Even now, the old omens remain. Drop a fork and expect a woman. Drop a knife and a man's coming. A spoon means someone you weren't expecting. If two people stir the same pot at once, they'll argue before sundown. If the biscuits won't rise, someone's lying or pregnant or both. If the kettle screams when the heat hasn't changed, something big is already on its way. It's a signal that sounds like a train whistle and there's no stopping its motion at that point. These aren't superstitions taken lightly. These wise people used them as alarm bells.

The meaning runs deeper than the sayings. A ladle used with focus carries emotion into food. A rolling pin pressed with care can knead peace into dough. Stirring a pot counterclockwise moves tension out of a room. A bay leaf added to soup can hold a name, a question, or a warning if you know how to read it once it floats. Bread can carry tokens baked right in— buttons for change, coins for luck, beans for uncertainty. The ingredients weren't just flavor. They were a forecast of things to come.

Eggs have a language of their own. A double yolk means something's doubling like a blessing, or trouble, or twins. A yolk that won't break means something's clinging. An egg that rolls off the counter without cracking means something passed you by that might have stuck if the timing had been wrong. None of this came from books. It came from watching what happened after the bread burned, or the spoon cracked, or the salt spilled twice in one hour.

The kitchen wasn't sacred because someone lit candles. It was sacred because everything met there—birth and grief, hunger and comfort, protection and release. It was where you could feed a child and whisper a name into the steam at the same time. Where you could hold back tears while cutting onions and let the knife carry the tension out. The work was layered, and the signs, when they appeared, were recognized by people who didn't need them explained.

They felt the air change. Smelled the wrongness in the steam. Heard the spoon fall and didn't call it coincidence. That's where real folk practice lives. Not in rhyming spells, but in the moment someone says, "That didn't fall right," and looks to the window to see who shows up.

You don't need a shelf of spellbooks to practice kitchen magic. You don't need moon charts or altar cloths. If you've ever stirred a pot and felt the air grow heavy, if you've smelled something burning before you saw smoke, if you've dropped a fork and said "Uh-oh" before you even knew why, you're already the kind of person who notices these things. That's the real foundation of kitchen magic. It isn't about ritual. It's about awareness. The kitchen doesn't care whether you believe in magic. It only asks if you're paying attention.

## THE MAGIC

Dropped utensils are one of the oldest forms of divination still in use. Not because anyone decided they should be, but because they kept showing up right before something happened. A fork hits the floor and someone's on the way. A knife jumps from the counter and tension's coming with teeth. A spoon lands bowl-down and spins in place—there's an unsettled visit ahead. The pattern isn't symbolic. It's behavioral. The tool mirrors the energy that's moving through the space.

As with most sympathetic work, the details matter: the direction the utensil points, whether it lands clean or tangled in the rug, whether it falls from your hand or jumps on its own. The utensil stands in as proxy. When it moves out of rhythm, something else is already moving behind it.

The same logic applies to the stove. Burned food, failed rising, pots that boil over after being turned down—these aren't kitchen mistakes. They're messages. If you've made the same cornbread every Sunday for years and one day it splits down the middle, you don't blame the oven. You look at who just walked in. If the biscuits stay flat no matter how fresh the flour is, you ask what's being hidden. Pregnancy. Lies. Grief that hasn't been spoken. The oven responds before anyone else does.

And then there's the pot. In older kitchens, there was

one rule about stirring: you don't let two people stir the same dish at the same time unless you want a fight. It isn't superstition. It's crossed energy. Two sets of hands move in opposite directions. The intentions pull apart. That gets cooked into the food. So does the direction of your stir: clockwise to draw something in: like calm, joy, peace, healing, strength. Counterclockwise to push something out: tension, illness, bitterness. It's a choice every time the spoon turns. And once it's stirred, you can't take the power back out.

That's why certain people were trusted to make the stew and others weren't. Not because of the recipe, but because of their presence.

Every herb in a kitchen carries a use beyond taste. Salt seals and protects. Tossing it over your left shoulder isn't just habit. It's a quick ward against whatever's brushed too close to you. Bay leaves hold names and questions. Black pepper cuts through confusion and deceit. Rosemary restores focus. Garlic clears the air. These aren't kitchen witchery clichés. They're practical systems that grew out of necessity. If you lived in a house where anger and worry traveled faster than news, you learned what to boil, what to burn, and what to bury.

Even the pantry speaks if you know how to listen. If the salt keeps disappearing, someone's talking about you. If the same spice keeps falling from the shelf, that's a signal to stop using it, or to use more of it, depending on the trouble. If food spoils overnight for no reason, the air in the house needs clearing. You don't need to prove it. You just need to clean it.

And then there's the knife. When a kitchen knife falls without cause, it isn't just clumsy hands. It marks a boundary breaking. Folk logic treats a fallen knife as a sign of intrusion, often from male energy or emotional disruption. Where it lands tells the rest of the story. Pointing at the door means someone's on the way. Embedded in the floor means unfinished work. If it strikes, bounces twice, and doesn't settle straight, that energy is mixed. Whoever arrives next might not realize what they're carrying.

When that happens, you don't announce it. You pick up the knife, rinse it under cold water, speak your name over it, and set it back with intention. That isn't ceremony. It's maintenance. You're resetting the charge. You're telling the kitchen, *I heard it. I'm responding.*

The deeper you look at these signs, the less random they seem. They're inherited. Not always by blood, but by proximity. You don't need someone to teach you what it means when a spoon falls twice in an hour. You only need to remember how your grandmother paused when it happened and how she swept the floor afterward without saying a word.

That's the shape of real domestic magic. It doesn't

perform. It just remembers. And when something feels off, it doesn't ask you to fix it. It asks you to notice. The rest happens from there.

In houses where the kitchen mattered, the warnings didn't arrive with noise. They showed up through what changed: the burner that didn't catch on the first try, the kettle that screamed at the wrong moment, the spoon that cracked even though the soup wasn't thick enough to fight back. And the people who knew didn't say anything right away. They just paid attention to what followed.

## THE SIGNS

There's a story from Georgia. A woman was boiling water like she did every day. Same kettle. Same burner. But that afternoon it didn't whistle. It screamed. Not the sound of steam or metal. Something else. Something that stopped her cold. She turned off the burner, checked the kettle, and found nothing wrong. But her hands were shaking, and the hairs on her arms stood up like a door had opened somewhere. Ten minutes later, the phone rang. Her daughter was in labor six weeks early. The baby was fine. Came quick. But the kettle never made that sound again.

That's how these things work. Sometimes the kitchen isn't warning you about something bad. It's warning you about something big. A change. Something crossing through.

In North Carolina, a woman burned a pan of biscuits she'd made every Sunday for twenty years. Same oven. Same pan. Same time. But that morning they came out black on the bottom and left a smell in the air like soot. That afternoon an old friend she hadn't seen in a decade knocked on her door. Said he was passing through and needed a place to stay. She poured coffee without missing a beat. When he said it smelled good, she nodded. "Burned the biscuits this morning," she told him. "Figured someone was coming." He laughed. She didn't. She slid the butter across the table and kept her eye on the stove.

Sometimes the sign isn't what happens. It's what won't stop. One house in the Ozarks wouldn't cool down after the grandmother died. Not in July. Not in December. The kitchen stayed hot all the time, like the oven was running even when it wasn't. The new owner blamed insulation, but the wiring checked out. The ducts were clear. The thermostat was fine. Then someone pulled the stove away from the wall and found her cast-iron skillet tucked behind it, still slightly greasy. Still warm. Like someone had finished cooking and walked off midmeal. They set a plate of food beside it and said her name out loud. The next morning, the kitchen was cool.

Another story. Simpler this time. A woman kept losing her salt. She'd set it on the counter and it would vanish. Show up in the laundry room one day and the next day, in the freezer. The day after that, on the porch. She told her aunt, who said, "Somebody's gossiping about you. Or you have about them." So she tossed the salt into the yard, swept the floor from back to front, and burned a match in every window. The salt stayed put after that. A few days later, she got a call from the exact person she hadn't been speaking kindly about.

These stories don't build toward a lesson. They don't wrap clean. They just tell what happened and what people did in response. The biscuits burned. The kettle screamed. The cast iron held its heat. The salt moved. And the people in the kitchen noticed.

The warning didn't come through a ghost. It came through a stovetop that wouldn't settle down. And the ones who understood didn't need a second sign.

Most kitchen magic doesn't begin with a candle. It begins with recognition—when something slips out of place and you know it wasn't carelessness. The spoon falls twice. The biscuits burn in the center but nowhere else. The salt moves again, though no one touched it. These aren't accidents. They're alerts. Once the room starts speaking, you either listen or you don't. And if you don't, the signs keep getting louder until you do.

## THE WORK

The first spell most people inherit without realizing it is the blessing bundle. You don't call it that. You just hang something behind the stove because your grandmother did. But if you know what goes in it, the work holds. Place one bay leaf, a pinch of salt, and a piece of garlic in a clean cloth. Tie it with red thread in three knots—no more, no less. Hang it where the heat from the oven can reach it without burning it. You don't need rhyme or ritual. You only need to speak clearly while you tie the thread: *Let this kitchen hold peace, and let anything that means harm turn back before it crosses the threshold.*

You don't touch the bundle again unless the kitchen feels off—if the air thickens, if the fire refuses to stay lit, if food spoils too soon. That's when you check it. If it's dry, brittle, or smells wrong, take it down and bury it with a handful of cornmeal. Then make another.

When utensils fall, the spell isn't in the tool. It's in the timing. If a fork jumps from the counter and something about it feels wrong, don't ignore it. Light a candle and set the fork beside it, handle pointing toward the nearest door. On a slip of paper, write the question that's been itching your thoughts—*Who's coming? What's this about?*—and slide it under a plate near the flame. Let the candle burn all the way down. Don't blow it out. Don't stop halfway.

While it burns, watch the flame. If it leans toward the fork, the energy coming in is familiar. If it leans away, you're dealing with someone or something you're not ready for. If it sputters or flickers too much to hold steady, the situation isn't settled yet. Wait before deciding anything. When the candle burns out, destroy the paper. You can burn it or bury it, but don't keep it. Clean the fork and put it away with intention. You're not predicting the future. You're reading the present while it's still warm.

If the kitchen feels wrong—if the stove doesn't sound like it used to, if the air thickens when you stir, if the food keeps turning bitter for no reason then it's time to reset the room. The simplest way is with a simmer pot. It doesn't need to be elaborate. Fill a pot with water, a handful of rosemary, a few strips of lemon peel, a bay leaf, and a splash of vinegar. Leave the lid off and let it roll at a gentle simmer while you clean the counters or sweep the floor. You don't need a chant. You just speak to the space while you work: *If anything here doesn't belong, let it lift and leave. If any energy's gone sour, let this clear it.* Let the pot run until the air smells clean and the room feels softer around the edges. When it's done, pour it out at the front step— not in the sink, not in the toilet. The door you walk through is the one that needs the clearing.

None of these spells are ornamental. You don't set them up for show. You do them when something shifts. The goal isn't performance. It's maintenance. If the room feels right when you finish, that's the proof. You don't need a sign. You don't wait for a knock.

A good kitchen holds memory. It holds pressure. It knows when a visitor's coming before the dog hears the car. It knows when someone's lying before their hand touches the doorknob. And if you pay attention, it shows you what's off—sometimes in the pot, sometimes in the bread, sometimes in the way the air won't clear no matter how wide you open the window.

When that happens, you don't light a candle and hope. You scrub the stove. You stir with purpose. You check the salt. And you trust the room that's kept your people fed to warn you when something's about to change.

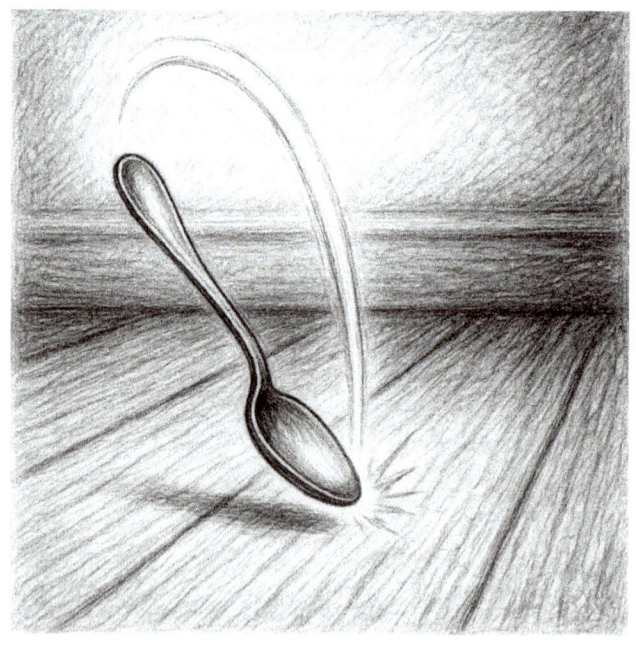

# THE MYRTLES PLANTATION - THE MIRROR THAT WATCHES

They say the Myrtles is beautiful until you stay too long. At first it feels like any old Southern house—wide porches, long halls, trees that lean in close as if they're listening. But after a few minutes inside, something in the quiet begins to press. You start watching the corners of rooms, paying attention to reflections, noticing where the air holds still. It's that sense of being observed that turns curiosity into caution.

There's a hallway in that old house in Louisiana where the light doesn't land quite right. It filters through high windows and hangs there like dust that's learned how to wait. The air feels thick even when the doors are open, and the sound of footsteps, real or imagined, travels farther than it should. The floors creak whether anyone's walking or not. The scent is a mix of polish and damp wood, the kind of smell that tells you a house has seen too many summers and not enough rest.

On the wall near the parlor hangs a large mirror framed in heavy gilt, made to impress company that never came. The glass is old, faintly rippled, the kind that holds light a little too long before letting it go. It's the sort of mirror that catches your attention without asking for it. People don't always look into it on purpose. Sometimes they just notice that something in the glass seems off. A faint smudge that won't wipe away. A reflection that doesn't quite match the room. A sense that someone passed behind them when no one did. Nothing dramatic. Just enough to make them look twice, and then look away.

Houses that carry grief develop their own gravity. Rooms remember. Wood holds breath. The longer sorrow stays, the more it sinks into the frame. The Myrtles is that kind of house. It's a place where the air itself feels watchful, where the quiet between rooms is thick enough to count as company.

In Southern mourning customs, mirrors are covered after a death. Not out of superstition, but to keep grief from trapping what's passing. The belief is simple: if a soul sees itself in glass before it fully lets go, it might not leave. At the Myrtles Plantation, they say one mirror wasn't covered—not after a death, not after what came next. And in a house like that, already heavy with sorrow and interruption, leaving a glass uncovered wasn't just carelessness. It was an opening.

## THE HISTORY

The Myrtles stands in St. Francisville, Louisiana. It's often called one of the most haunted houses in the country, though that depends on what you mean by haunted. The stories there are plenty: the girl in the turban, the man shot on the stairs, the children. But what most people talk about isn't what they saw. It's what they felt. Visitors rarely describe ghosts. They describe pressure. The sense of being watched. Standing in front of a mirror and not quite getting their face back.

The house was built in 1796 by General David Bradford, best known for helping lead the Whiskey

Rebellion before fleeing Pennsylvania and starting over in what was then Spanish territory. He called the estate Laurel Grove. He rebuilt his life and was eventually pardoned by the U.S. government. Like most men of his rank, his wealth rested on land and labor that weren't his. The property was worked by enslaved people—a truth that seldom makes the brochures.

After Bradford's death, the house passed to his daughter Sarah Matilda and her husband, Judge Clark Woodruff. Woodruff had a reputation for being strict and ambitious. During his time at the Myrtles, Sarah and two of their daughters died. It was most likely from yellow fever, which struck the South often in those years. But as time moves on, certainty fades. And in a house where people already believe the air holds on to what it shouldn't, speculation grows fast.

The property changed hands several times. In the 1830s, it was bought by the Sterling family, who turned it into the Greek Revival showpiece it remains today with its marble mantels, carved staircases, and all the grandeur visitors seem to admire. Then came the Civil War. Some say Union soldiers died on the grounds. Others say they vanished. Either way, the land didn't reset. By the late 1800s, the Myrtles had already gathered generations of death, disease, and sorrow. That's when the stories began to take form and take on an eerie tone.

One of the most familiar names tied to the house is Chloe. No census record lists her. No birth or death certificate confirms her. But folklore doesn't always need paperwork. The story says Chloe was an enslaved woman in the Woodruff household. One day she was caught standing outside a door listening to a conversation. As punishment, Judge Woodruff ordered her ear cut off. After that, she wore a green turban to hide the wound. Some versions claim she was forced into a relationship with the Judge. Others call it an affair, but back then there wasn't equality in those situations. It wasn't romance. It was survival.

Fearing she might be cast out, Chloe is said to have baked a cake mixed with oleander which is poisonous and common to find. The plan, legend says, was to make the family sick enough that she could nurse them back to health and prove her worth. But it failed. The Judge's wife and two daughters died. The Judge lived. The other enslaved people, afraid of collective punishment, hanged Chloe and threw her body into the river.

No record supports this. No newspaper mention. No official evidence that a woman named Chloe lived or died on that land. But her story lasts despite there being no documents. Guests claim to see a woman in a green head wrap walking the halls. Earrings go missing—always from the left ear. People feel watched in empty rooms. They see motion in the mirror. A story like that doesn't need proof to survive.

It only needs to be told.

Another death the house is known for is that of William Drew Winter, who married into the Sterling family. In 1871, he was shot on the front porch. The story says he dragged himself back inside and up the staircase before collapsing on the seventeenth step. Visitors still count them. Some say they hear footsteps that stop there. Others say they feel drawn to that step without knowing why. Whether the details are true or not has stopped mattering. The house holds the story so it gets told and retold.

And then there's the mirror—the one said to have been left uncovered after a death in the house. The one visitors still hesitate to face for too long. They clean it, and the smudges come back. Handprints. Small. Low on the glass, like a child pressed their palms there. Some say their reflection lags. Some say it shifts. Some say it looks like it's standing in another room altogether.

Whatever the cause, whatever the name, the mirror remains where it's always been. In a house that's known so much loss and unfinished grief, the thought that one pane of glass might still be holding something doesn't seem far-fetched. People stand before it and walk away changed. They look at the photos they took days later. They cover their own mirrors when they get home. Not because they believe in ghosts, but because their instincts said to.

## THE MAGIC

Mirrors aren't neutral. In folk magic, they don't just reflect. They respond. They don't take sides, but they don't stay empty either. A mirror shows what stands before it, yet it also absorbs the energy of everything that's ever moved through its view. And when the conditions are right, that energy can stay.

You'll find mirrors used in magical work across many regions and systems: Appalachian, hoodoo, Afro-Caribbean, European folk practice, even ceremonial paths that rarely agree on anything. What all of them share is the understanding that mirrors act as both tools and thresholds. They can reflect, return, store, amplify, or open.

In most Southern and Appalachian homes, mirrors don't receive special attention unless something shifts in the air. But in magical households, they're handled with care. As we've talked about before, when someone dies, the mirrors are covered—not from superstition, but from caution. A soul that hasn't fully detached can see itself in the glass and get caught, because to a spirit, it's a door that's been left open. And once it's open, it doesn't always close on its own.

Unsealed mirrors are sometimes called thin places. The phrase gets used loosely, but here it fits. It means the mirror has become a point where the boundary between the physical and the spiritual has worn thin. That can happen through trauma, grief, neglect, ritual, or simply time. If someone dies in front of a mirror and no one seals it afterward, the glass doesn't just remember. It holds the residue of that crossing. It keeps the echo of that moment open until someone tells it otherwise.

In hoodoo, mirrors are used for return work. A practitioner will take the name of the person causing harm and place it behind a small mirror that's been cleaned, charged, and fixed for reversal. The mirror is then hidden, sometimes under a bed, sometimes behind a cabinet, but always facing inward. Any energy sent toward the client reflects back to its source. This isn't symbolic. It's mechanical. The glass acts as the engine. It doesn't choose what to return. It simply mirrors what arrives, whether that's malice, hexes, interference, or unwanted attention. It can also return grief, confusion, fear, or the residue of a lingering presence.

That's why mirrors become dangerous when they've been left open too long. They magnify. They return. They hold. If a room carries heavy history like fighting, death, loss, or magical work done without closure and a mirror has been sitting in the middle of it, that mirror stops being decoration. It becomes a vessel that stores everything the room couldn't process.

There are signs when a mirror is holding too much. You clean it, and the same smudges reappear. You feel watched when you walk past, even without looking into it. Animals act wary or unsettled. Children either avoid it or stare for too long. Sometimes your reflection lags or moves out of rhythm with your body. These aren't cinematic ghost signs. They're subtle, and they usually come with a weight in the air, like the room is waiting for something to finish that never quite did.

Sealing a mirror isn't difficult, but it must be done with intention. Start by cleaning the surface with something spiritually active: Florida Water, salt and rue water, or vinegar steeped with rosemary, depending on your system. Then speak aloud—not a chant, not a performance—just a statement that sets the rule: *This mirror reflects only what is mine to see. Nothing else is welcome here.* After that, cover the mirror with black cloth. Wrap the frame in red thread, three turns and three knots. A small iron piece, such as a nail or key, can be placed or taped to the back. If the air still feels heavy, sprinkle black salt or crushed eggshell along the base.

That seals the mirror for a time. If the room still feels unsettled after several days, the mirror may need to be moved or stored. Some mirrors were never meant to remain uncovered. Some need to be placed face-down and left alone. That isn't superstition. It's spiritual hygiene. A tool built to hold power can also hold residue, and when that residue isn't cleared, it keeps breathing.

Mirrors also appear in active work. Setting a candle before a mirror doubles its light and doubles its reach—a simple way to strengthen a blessing or a call-in spell. In scrying practice, a darkened mirror becomes a surface for gazing. The worker looks into the reflection until an image, message, or sensation rises to meet them. That kind of work isn't casual. It requires training, a clean space, and a clear purpose. You don't stare into a mirror to see what appears. You approach it with a question and a boundary.

What happened at the Myrtles, the mirror left uncovered after a death, is the kind of oversight that lingers long after a house changes hands. A death. An open mirror. Years of grief, confusion, and layered spiritual residue. And no one sealing the glass. That's how a mirror starts to watch back. Not because it's cursed, but because no one ever forced it to stop.

## THE SIGNS

The Myrtles doesn't tell one ghost story. It tells dozens of small ones. Some appear on plaques or in tour scripts. Others pass quietly between staff and visitors who never believed in anything until a hallway made them reconsider. People talk about Chloe. They talk about the seventeenth step. But the stories that hold weight are the quieter ones—told secondhand by someone who stayed too long in front of a mirror or found themselves avoiding one corner of the house without knowing why.

One of the most common reports involves earrings. Always the left one. Visitors say they wore a pair into the house and left with one missing. The backing was secure. They hadn't brushed against anything. They didn't notice until later—on the way out, back at the hotel, or while undressing for bed. Some find the earring later in places that make no sense like a shoe they haven't worn or the pocket of a jacket left in the car. Others never find it. No one's been harmed, but the pattern repeats often enough to notice. Some call it Chloe's doing, a nod to the story of her ear. Others call it a signature of something small, specific, and impossible to ignore.

There's another story about a young girl seen at the foot of a guest bed. She doesn't move or speak. She just stands there barefoot, looking like someone from an old photograph that no one passes around anymore. She disappears the moment you look away or your focus slips. No one knows who she is. She doesn't match any of the children named in the records, but her presence is described the same way each time. Small dress. Quiet eyes. A feeling like you once knew her name but can't recall it now.

The staircase still carries its own memories. The story of William Winter being shot on the porch, pulling himself inside, and collapsing on the seventeenth step is the kind of tale that stays whether or not it's been confirmed. Visitors count the steps every time. Some say they hear dragging footsteps that stop too soon.

Others say their body hesitates on that step without knowing why. The house doesn't perform the story. It just refuses to let go of it.

But it's the mirror people talk about when they're back home. One woman said she stood in front of it and couldn't blink. Her reflection kept eye contact longer than she could. Another said she saw a hallway in the glass that didn't match the one behind her. A man leaned in to fix his collar and saw someone standing behind him who wasn't there. Not a shadow. Not a face. Just presence. Enough to make him step back and avoid that part of the house for the rest of his visit.

A guest once said she leaned in to check her makeup, and as she exhaled, a handprint appeared in the fog right in front of her. Child-sized. Still. Perfectly clear. She covered every mirror in her house for a week after she got home. Not because she thought for certain the Myrtles had sent something with her, but because she wanted to be absolutely sure it hadn't followed.

It is said that the staff at the Myrtles have their own ways of keeping balance. Some wear iron jewelry. Some keep salt packets in their pockets. One former guide said if you open a door in that hallway, you close it again immediately. No exceptions. Once, someone forgot, and the next morning every door in that wing stood open the same small amount. No wind. No damage. Just precision, like something had walked through with intent.

No one says it aloud during the tours, but most agree that the mirror isn't haunted in the theatrical sense. It doesn't show faces. It doesn't shift rooms. It doesn't throw objects. What it does is hold energy. It holds the charge of grief, fear, and unfinished memory. It waits for recognition.

It's the kind of haunted object that doesn't need to act to unsettle you. It doesn't perform tricks. It simply absorbs energy and information. And if you stand in front of it too long, it will start reflecting all those secrets you're carrying right back at you.

There's nothing sentimental about a mirror that's taken on too much. It doesn't ask for attention or offer an explanation. It stays charged. Once it's crossed that threshold of being exposed to death, grief, magical work, or long neglect it doesn't go back to being ordinary glass. It may not show anything clear. Most never do. But you'll feel it: a pause when you walk past, a flicker that doesn't belong, a pull in your body that says you're not alone even when you are. That isn't imagination. It's residual power looking for a surface to settle in.

## THE WORK

If you have a mirror that feels active—whether it came from an antique store, an inheritance, or began feeling wrong after a death or an argument—the first step is to shut it down. Not with fear. Not with drama. With discipline. Start by cleaning the glass, not with commercial cleaner but with something that clears: Florida Water, saltwater, or a rosemary wash. Wipe the frame as well. Then speak directly to it. Don't rhyme. Don't perform. Just state the boundary: *This mirror reflects only what is mine to see. Anything else is released.*

After that, cover it fully with black cloth. Wrap the entire frame, not just the glass. Wind red thread around the cloth three times and knot it once at the end. Place a small iron object behind the mirror like a nail, a key, or a working blade already tied to your practice. Iron doesn't cleanse. It grounds. It seals the door that's been left open. If the mirror has been pulling power for years, grounding is what it needs most.

If the room still feels unsettled, add a pinch of black salt or crushed eggshell to the windowsill or beneath a piece of furniture. Leave the mirror covered for one full moon cycle. If the air lightens, the work is complete. If it doesn't, move the mirror out of the room, turn it to face the wall, or bury it in the earth. Don't break it. Don't burn it. Just close it.

When you visit a place like the Myrtles or any site heavy with history, grief, or spiritual residue, you don't need to walk in armored, but you do need to walk in aware. You don't owe the space your trust, and you don't owe whatever lingers there a chance to follow you back home. That's what protection bundles are for.

To make one, combine salt, rosemary, and a clean piece of cloth that hasn't been used for anything else. Add your breath to it—just a steady exhale with intent and tie it shut with black thread. Carry it on your person. Not as decoration. As insurance. When you return home, don't set it aside. Dispose of it. Bury it at a crossroads, drop it in running water, or burn it if you must. Never keep it as a souvenir. Its work ended the moment you left the property safely.

The point of all this isn't fear. It's protocol. Mirrors aren't evil. They're engines. They perform the function they were made for: to reflect, to echo, to amplify what's set before them. In houses like the Myrtles, these places where things aren't resolved, where rooms go spiritually uncleansed, and where mirrors stay uncovered after death—the energy they hold onto can be subtle. Sometimes it lingers, waiting for someone to come along and recognize it.

That's why the stories persist. Not because the ghosts are loud, but because something in the glass keeps noticing whoever looks too long. And when you feel that awareness turning back toward you, that's when you cover the mirror, speak your boundary aloud, and step away.

# BOTTLE TREES AND THE SPIRITS THEY CATCH

At the edge of a small yard, the kind where the fence has begun to lean and the grass no longer remembers its pattern, a tree stands dressed in glass. Bottles hang from every branch: some clear, some the color of river water, and some a deep cobalt that turns almost black when the sun drops behind it. They move when the wind moves, and when they strike one another they make a sound that sits between chime and warning. People who don't know what they're looking at call it decoration. People who do pause before they walk past.

The bottles aren't there for beauty. They're there for boundary. Each one is a ward, a trap, a promise that whatever wanders through that yard uninvited will find itself distracted by the glint and the hollow rattle, drawn inside the narrow mouth of the glass and held there until morning. When the sun rises, the light burns through the bottle and clears whatever was caught. What remains of the spirit, the shadow, or the thought that didn't belong becomes nothing but heat in the air.

That's how the story is told, and like most that have survived this long, there's truth built into it. The bottle tree isn't a Southern invention, though the South claims it now. It's an inheritance, one carried across the Atlantic not by choice but by endurance. Its first form can be traced to Central and West Africa, to the Bakongo and neighboring peoples who understood glass, especially blue glass, as more than material.

In Bakongo cosmology there is a river that divides the living from the ancestral world. The surface of that water is where reflection lives. It shimmers, it bends light, and it confuses direction. Blue glass mimics that barrier. To possess it, or to hang it in the air, is to build a piece of the boundary at home.

In those same systems of belief, sound and reflection distract spirits that have lost their way. A bright shimmer, a metallic rattle, even the sudden motion of air can pull an unsettled spirit toward it. The bottle, narrow at the neck and hollow inside, became a perfect trap. Once the spirit followed the light or the sound into the opening, the confusion of echoes and curves kept it there. What could not be banished could still be contained.

## THE HISTORY

When Africans were forced into the Americas through the slave trade, they carried this knowledge with them. Shrines and carved symbols could be forbidden or destroyed, but the practice of using glass and sound as defense survived because it could pass for decoration. A row of bottles placed along a fence or hanging from a bare tree might look harmless to an overseer. To the one who built it, it was protection hidden in plain sight.

That adaptation is how the bottle tree took root in the American South. It grew from necessity and secrecy, a tradition that had to disguise itself to keep living. The tree most often chosen was cedar, myrtle, or crepe myrtle—something sturdy enough to hold bottles without blooming too heavy in spring. The bottles were inverted so their mouths faced down or out, never up, because spirits are lured into openings; they don't climb. Most of the time, the tree was stripped of leaves so nothing shaded the glass. Sunlight had to reach the bottles in the morning, to burn out whatever the night had drawn in.

In Gullah-Geechee culture, the same work took on a name of its own. The restless spirits that drift and cause trouble were called *haints*, a word descended from *haunt* but reshaped by dialect and time. A haint isn't a demon. It's a soul that has missed its road, a ghost that doesn't realize it's dead, or one that clings to a grievance until it can't move on. You don't bargain with a haint. You trick it. You give it something shiny, something noisy, something confusing. The haint spends the night circling what it thinks is a doorway and never finds the threshold it was looking for.

That's the same reasoning behind haint-blue porch ceilings. Spirits cross where color looks like water. Paint the ceiling that shade and they move upward instead of inward. Hang bottles in the yard and they follow the glint, never finding the porch. The logic is consistent: redirect, don't wrestle. Let the trick do the work.

As the generations shifted, bottle trees became fixtures in Black Southern yards. They stood by gates and porches, near crossroads, and along the outer edge of gardens. The materials changed with whatever was at hand: wine bottles, medicine jars, milk glass, but the core remained blue. Blue confuses the dead. Blue feels like distance. A cobalt bottle hanging in the wind is a small piece of sky pretending to be water. Spirits move toward it and forget what they meant to do.

By the early twentieth century, the practice had spread beyond its original communities. Poor white Southerners adopted it, sometimes knowing what it was, sometimes not. WPA folklore collectors in the 1930s recorded bottle trees across Mississippi and Alabama, with informants explaining that the bottles "keep the haints away" or simply "keep things quiet." Others insisted they were just for looks, but the reluctance to take them down told the truth. A decoration doesn't get treated like that.

Over time the bottle tree drifted into mainstream visibility. Magazines rebranded it as folk art. Hardware stores sold welded metal "trees" with matching blue bottles for gardeners who wanted a rustic touch. The meaning dimmed but never disappeared. Even stripped of language, the form still functions. Color, sound, light, and air continue to work whether or not the maker remembers the theology behind them. A boundary doesn't stop being a boundary because the sign fell off.

Within African American communities that kept closer ties to conjure and ancestral practice, bottle trees also evolved into altars. Each bottle could stand for a relative or a prayer. Some were left open to feed the dead with song and sunlight. Some were sealed to contain grief. In this version, the tree no longer traps, it tends. The purpose shifted from defense to remembrance, but the mechanism stayed the same: a vessel that catches what shouldn't wander loose.

## THE MAGIC

Today you can find bottle trees everywhere from plantation museums that tell only half the story to suburban yards that don't realize they're telling one. But under the surface gloss, the original purpose still hums. A bottle tree is a spiritual machine. It takes the restlessness of the unseen world and gives it shape, color, and place. It keeps movement where it belongs and peace where people live.

A bottle tree looks harmless until you understand how it's built. To most people it's just a handful of blue glass catching the light, something that moves when the wind moves. But to the person who made it with intention, it's a magical working that never shuts off. Each bottle is a spell that that runs on air and sound instead of candle flame.

The logic is older than language. Spirits travel along currents of power the way birds ride thermals. They move where motion draws them. The shimmer of sunlight through colored glass, the small clink when the wind hits, the reflection that never quite holds still—these are invitations to whatever drifts between worlds. The spirit moves toward what shines. Once it reaches the mouth of the bottle, the shape does the rest. Wide at the base, narrow at the throat. It pulls the presence inward, then confuses it with its own echo. The thing that entered to investigate can't find its way out again. The sound that follows—a hollow vibration when there shouldn't be any wind is the spell reporting back that it's working.

Blue glass is chosen for a reason. Blue mimics the surface of water, which in many African-rooted cosmologies marks the line between the living and the dead. The color convinces restless power that it has reached that crossing. It pauses there, content to stay. The same principle drives the haint-blue porch ceilings still seen across the South. Paint the ceiling blue and the spirit looks up, believes it's met water or sky, and moves on. Hang blue bottles and you give that illusion depth. The light shifts through the glass like moving water. The haint follows and gets caught.

The sound is just as important as the color. In folk magic, vibration carries intention. Bells, chimes, rattles, drums all break up stagnant air and drive power in a direction. A bottle tree uses that same rule. The gentle clatter of glass against glass does more than mark the wind. It keeps the air alive around the boundary of the home. Spirits are drawn to rhythm, but once they arrive, they find themselves enclosed. The bottles hum like a net made of musical notes. It's simple physics doing spiritual work.

Placement decides the strength of the spell. A bottle tree tucked behind the shed is quiet magic. One planted near the porch or along the road is active defense. The entrance of a property is where movement passes through most often, so that's where the trap belongs. Some workers face their trees east so the morning light can cleanse what was caught overnight. Others build them near crossroads where traffic, both physical and spiritual, runs heavy. The bottles don't need constant tending, but they need to be seen. A forgotten spell weakens; a watched one stays alive.

When a bottle breaks, you don't treat it as trash. You treat it as the end of a contract. The glass has done its job and released what it held. You gather the pieces carefully, wrap them in cloth, and bury them. Never throw them in the garbage or recycle bin. The act of burial seals what's finished. The tree then asks for renewal. You replace the missing bottle with one that's been cleaned in saltwater or Florida Water and spoken over. That's how the cycle keeps moving without interruption.

Not every bottle tree is made to trap. Some are made to honor. In those trees, the bottles aren't empty. They hold tokens like paper with names, dried herbs, bits of tobacco, a drop of whiskey. Those are offerings, not bait. The bottles become houses for ancestors, places where memory can rest. The tree is still a boundary, but it's a gate with permission built in. Spirits that belong to the family can visit. Strangers stay outside.

Every few months, or whenever the air around the tree starts feeling heavy, a small renewal spell keeps it balanced. A candle is lit at the base, a circle of crushed eggshell or brick dust is drawn around it, and a few words are spoken aloud—nothing ornate, just gratitude and acknowledgment. The point is to remind the bottles they're being seen. Glass that's respected protects better than glass that's ignored.

And there are rules. You don't take bottles from another person's tree. You don't hang empty bottles near a cemetery unless the work demands it. You don't set up a bottle tree indoors where spirits can't pass freely. And if you ever hear the bottles clinking when the air is still, you don't break the silence with chatter. You listen. That's the spell reporting in.

A bottle tree is the perfect example of how a spell can live in plain sight. No one calls it ritual. No one questions it. It just stands there bright and humming, catching what shouldn't cross the line. And when the wind hits right and the bottles rattle soft and even, that's the sound of a spell still doing exactly what it was made to do.

## THE SIGNS

The stories people tell about bottle trees don't come with jump scares. They're more like stories about little warnings to look for. The glass doesn't need words. It uses sound, motion, and coincidence to make its point. And the people who live with those trees learn quickly that paying attention is easier than ignoring them.

In northern Alabama, there's a family that still talks about the bottle tree their grandmother kept beside the chicken yard. It wasn't decorative. It was a stripped cedar trunk with a dozen cobalt bottles wired to the limbs. Whenever someone in the family got sick, three bottles would fall. Never more. Never less. They started counting the gaps in the tree the way other families count lightning strikes. When their uncle suffered a stroke, three bottles were on the ground before the ambulance came. When their cousin started seeing shadows in the hallway, three bottles broke before dawn. They never asked the tree to stop. They just replaced the bottles one by one, in silence, and thanked it for the warning.

Down in the Delta, another story circulates about a bottle tree that went still after its owner's funeral. The woman had been known for her sharp tongue and strong coffee, and the sound of her bottles rattling was part of the neighborhood. After she passed, her daughter left the tree exactly as it was, expecting it to keep singing in the wind. Within a week the air around it went flat. Even during a storm, the glass didn't move. The neighbors said the tree had followed its maker into the quiet. Finally, a friend walked a circle around it with salt and red brick dust. That night the wind came back, and the bottles whispered again. No one said what they thought had been caught inside the silence, but the daughter has kept the tree clean ever since.

In rural Georgia, an older man tells about the night a bottle tree called his name. He was a boy, sitting on the porch with his uncle, when the bottles started bumping against one another without a breeze. Between the clinks he heard a sound that shaped itself into his name. He went inside, couldn't sleep for two nights, and on the third day his cousin showed up unannounced—fresh out of jail, carrying trouble that stayed for a week and left behind a mess. When he told his uncle later, the old man said, "The tree wasn't talking to me. It was warning you." He keeps a bottle tree of his own now, and every time it stirs after dark, he listens before he moves.

Sometimes the tree refuses change. In South Carolina, a woman tried to modernize her grandmother's bottle tree. The old bottles were pale blue and sea-green, chipped but still holding. She replaced them with new amber glass, brighter, cleaner, all bought on the same day. Within a week three shattered on their own. The rest fogged from the inside, collecting condensation even in dry weather. She took them down, hung the old ones back, and the air cleared overnight. She didn't try again. Some spells recognize the hands that built them and don't take orders from strangers.

And every once in a while, a tree loses a bottle in a way no one can explain. One man in Mississippi had kept his tree for a decade without a crack. Then one morning a bottle was gone. Not broken. Not lying in the grass. Gone. The wire still twisted tight around an empty limb. That night his dog wouldn't step onto the porch. The next morning small bare footprints showed in the dew, circling the tree once and stopping beneath the missing branch. He lit a candle, scattered salt, and hung a new bottle before sunrise. The dog relaxed. The tree rattled once and went still. He never spoke about it again.

None of these stories sound dramatic when you first hear them. They sound like weather, like coincidence. But when the same shapes repeat with bottles falling in threes, trees going silent after death, new glass refusing old posts it stops being coincidence and becomes a pattern. That's what makes folk magic live. The bottle tree doesn't ask to be believed. It asks to be noticed. And the people who notice tend to stay safer than the ones who don't.

## THE WORK

A bottle tree is one of the few spells that can live outdoors all year and still keep working. It doesn't need a candle to stay lit or a prayer to stay alive. It only needs to stand where the wind can move through it. The glass and the air do the rest. When the breeze hits, the bottles knock together, and that sound becomes the heartbeat of the work like a steady rhythm that keeps the boundary strong. Folks call it decoration, but it's one of the oldest protections ever carried from one continent to another.

Start with intention before you ever reach for materials. Decide what the tree is for. If it's meant for defense, hang the bottles open and empty so they can catch what doesn't belong. If it's for remembrance, fill them with names on paper, a sprig of herb, a few drops of liquor. The same tree can't do both. Choose before you begin, because the glass remembers the first words spoken over it.

Once the purpose is clear, clean the bottles inside and out. Dirt dulls the light, and leftover energy from other hands clouds the work. Salt water, Florida Water, or vinegar steeped with rosemary will do. Rinse each bottle and talk to it while you work: *You'll hold what the wind brings. You'll keep what's not meant for me.* Words said once with focus are worth more than any rhyme or verse.

Next comes placement. A bottle tree works best where the air moves and where spirits pass such as by a porch, a gate, a road, or a crossroads. Set the post firm in the ground so it won't sway, then hang the bottles one at a time, upside down, mouths facing outward or down. The wind should be able to slip through them easy. Blue glass is best; it mimics water, and spirits mistake it for a boundary they can't cross. Green and clear glass work fine if that's what you have. As each bottle goes up, speak the same phrase. *You catch what wanders. You keep what stays too long.* By the time the last one's hung, the rhythm of your words has sealed the work tighter than any knot.

When the tree is finished, walk around it once clockwise and scatter a handful of crushed eggshell, salt, or brick dust at the base. That ties the work to the ground. You don't need to feed it or talk to it. Just notice it now and then. That's what keeps it alive.

A bottle tree doesn't wear out, but it can tire. When a bottle breaks, don't treat it like trash. The spell in that glass has done its job. Gather the pieces carefully, wrap them in black cloth, and bury them away from the house. Then replace the bottle with one that's been cleaned and spoken over, or leave the branch bare awhile if the air feels settled. A tree that hums too loud may start to draw more than it can handle. Balance keeps the work clean.

If the tree ever goes quiet and the air feels flat, it may be full of old, unspent energy. Wake it gently. Light a candle at the base and let the wax drip into the soil while you hang one new bottle. Sprinkle salt water around the roots and say, *Wind moves. Light clears. This tree works again.* That's enough to set it right.

If you move to a new house and can't take the tree, close it before you go. Remove the bottles one at a time, rinse them, and thank them. Wrap the trunk in cloth, walk a circle counterclockwise, and say, *This place keeps its peace. My protection travels with me.* Take one bottle from the old tree and hang it on the new. The spirit of the work will follow the sound.

And if you ever find someone else's bottle tree—old, weathered, still rattling when there's no wind just leave it alone. You don't know what it's holding, and you don't need to find out. Some works are personal. Some are family. The bottle tree can be both.

A bottle tree doesn't need to look magical to be powerful. Its beauty lies in how quietly it does the job. When the wind stirs the glass and the bottles chime, that's protection at work. Whatever spirit meant to cross your door is spinning in the light now confused by color, undone by sound, gone by morning.

That's the truth buried in all of it: real magic doesn't need attention to work. It just needs to be understood. The bottle tree never calls itself a spell, but it is one. It stands at the edge of the yard, humming in the sun, catching what doesn't belong and letting the rest pass through untouched.

So when you hear the bottles sing on a still night, don't make a wish and don't make a joke. Just listen.

Nod once. Say quietly, *Good work.* Then go back inside and let the tree keep watch.

In the Appalachian hills, blue bottles weren't always hung on trees. Long before the bottle tree took root in Southern yards, folks kept single bottles in their windowsills to guard the house from wandering spirits. Blue glass was thought to confuse the restless dead—the color reminded them of water, a boundary they couldn't cross. Sunlight through that glass made a barrier as real as any prayer. Some said the spirit, seeing its reflection caught in the bottle's curve, would mistake it for a doorway and stay there until morning light burned it away. Whether people called it superstition or sense, the rule held steady: a blue bottle in the window meant the living were keeping watch.

# THE HEX MURDER
# OF YORK COUNTY

The trees in York County lose their leaves early. By the end of November, the hills look stripped bare, every branch a line against a sky the color of tin. The air smells of wood smoke and frost, but out on the back roads there's only silence and the slow crunch of dirt under boot soles. One of those roads runs to a two-story farmhouse that sits uneven on its foundation, the kind of place that grew a little at a time—an extra room here, a lean-to there, until nothing quite matched. Tonight one lamp burns in the window. The chimney is cold. No sound carries from inside.

The man who lives there, Nelson Rehmeyer, isn't a stranger to anyone in these hills. He's been here all his life. People come to him when the doctor's done all he can, when a cow goes dry, when a baby won't stop crying. They say he can *powwow*—that old Pennsylvania Dutch blend of prayer, herbs, and charm work that keeps small communities stitched together when nothing else will. Rehmeyer works quietly. He doesn't advertise. He doesn't take advantage. He reads from his Bible, speaks the right words, and something eases. That's enough for most folks.

The same reputation that draws people to a healer can turn on him without warning. A man who can cure a fever can cause one. A man who can bless a field can blight it. That's what folks whisper after they thank him: respect what he does, but don't cross him.

That night three men come up the road to Nelson Rehmeyer's house. One's just a boy. One's John Blymire, already half-haunted by his own thinking.

He's sure Rehmeyer's hexed him. They've brought rope, matches, and a plan that sounds, in their heads, like salvation.

Rehmeyer lets them in. He always does. They sit at his kitchen table, eat a little bread, talk small. Then the talk burns off and something mean takes its place. When it's done, Rehmeyer's on the floor. They try to set the house on fire, to burn his body and the book they think holds his power, but the flames won't take. The smoke climbs a little way up the wall and dies out. They run into the dark.

It's 1928. Telephones hang on farmhouse walls, radios hum with sermons and ball scores, but out here the old ways still run deep. *Powwow*, the Pennsylvania Dutch mix of Bible verses, herbs, and charm-work hasn't faded yet. It sits right beside Christianity, not under it. And where there's healing, there's fear. Folks figure if the same words that stop bleeding can stop a heart, then a healer's gift cuts both ways.

That's what built this tragedy: belief strong enough to heal, turned backward until it made a man think killing was a cure.

## THE HISTORY

By the time Nelson Rehmeyer was killed, *powwow* had been part of rural Pennsylvania life for generations. The phrase "Pennsylvania Dutch" hides the truth; these weren't Dutch immigrants but *Deutsch*—

German Protestants from the Palatinate, Switzerland, and nearby regions who came in the eighteenth century carrying their language, their almanacs, and their quiet mix of faith and superstition. They built farms in the limestone valleys, spoke dialects that blended High German and English, and kept the old customs that softened daily life: weather signs, healing charms, protective marks carved into barn doors.

Within that mix grew *braucherei*—the practice later called *powwow*. It wasn't witchcraft in their eyes. It was useful Christianity, a way to handle sickness and bad luck when the doctor was twenty miles away and prayer was the only medicine you could afford. A *braucher*, or powwow doctor, healed sprains with whispered verses, stopped bleeding with psalms, and eased nightmares with paper charms tucked under the pillow. His authority came from Scripture, not secrecy, and that made the work acceptable in a community that would never have tolerated open magic.

Much of the system was gathered into a small book printed in Reading, Pennsylvania, in 1820—*The Long Lost Friend* by John George Hohman. It promised protection from thieves, safety while traveling, cures for fever, and blessings for livestock. Every charm was framed as prayer: "Speak these words and have faith in God, and it shall be so." To own the book was to own a tool. To misuse it was to invite trouble. Copies passed from hand to hand until the bindings gave out. Nearly every family in York and Lancaster counties had seen one.

In that world, Nelson Rehmeyer wasn't an oddity. He was ordinary and just one of several local men known for healing. He treated animals and people alike, asked little payment, and lived alone in a hollow that still carries his name. But even ordinary healers can be considered suspicious in a place where everything divides into help or harm. For every person who swore he was blessed, another muttered that he meddled with things better left alone.

John Blymire grew up with those beliefs. His parents practiced *powwow*, he learned the same verses, the same herbs. As a boy he was frail and unlucky, and folks told his family he'd been crossed. The explanation fit too neatly to question. Through his teens and into manhood, whenever misfortune hit, someone repeated the story that a curse was on him, laid by another practitioner. He went from one powwow doctor to the next, and for a time the remedies helped. But the peace never lasted.

By the 1920s Blymire was a man adrift, working odd jobs and certain that unseen hands were sabotaging him. The belief hardened into obsession. Another healer told him the spell could be broken only if he found the one who'd hexed him and burned that person's *hex book* along with a lock of hair. Burn them together, the man said, and the tie would die. On paper, it was an old European working meant to cut psychic bonds. In practice, it was a recipe for blame.

Somewhere in that spiral of fear, Blymire fixed on Nelson Rehmeyer. Maybe because Rehmeyer was respected. Maybe because he stood for the mastery Blymire never found. In folk communities, envy and dread often share the same face. Blymire started telling people that the older man was draining his strength, wrecking his fortune, twisting his thoughts.

He found two others willing to believe him: John Curry, a factory worker who couldn't shake his own run of bad luck, and Milton Hess, only fourteen. Each saw in Blymire's plan a way to shove misfortune somewhere else. Together they decided to confront the powwow doctor and take what they thought was the heart of his power.

On November 27 they crossed the fields to Nelson Rehmeyer's farmhouse. He welcomed them, offered food, and sat them at his table. They talked a while. Then the talk turned, and fear took over. They demanded his book. He refused. They attacked.

The rest is guesswork. When the neighbors found him beaten to death two days later, the kitchen was scorched and the air still thick with smoke. The book they came for was never found.

The papers called it the York County Hex Murder. To outsiders it was proof that old-world superstition still clung to the Pennsylvania Dutch like barn dust. For the people who lived there, it was shame. The trial records show how hard the defense tried to make it sound like madness instead of belief. Blymire told the court he'd been under a spell and meant only to free himself. The jury didn't see it that way. He got life. Curry and Hess got long terms. All three were later released, but the word *powwow* wasn't spoken out loud in that part of Pennsylvania for years.

After 1928, *braucherei* slipped underground. Well, at least in that area. The healers kept working, but quiet now. Folks came after dark. The prayers were whispered, not recited. What had been a respected Christian folk practice turned secret, almost suspect. In that silence the Rehmeyer story became both warning and myth. The hollow kept his name, and the house was rebuilt.

People say the air around it carries a different weight, like the land remembers all the bad things that happened there.

## THE MAGIC

It's easy to frame this story as superstition turned violent when a few desperate men believed in curses they couldn't prove. But that's too simple. What happened in Rehmeyer's Hollow isn't about ignorance. It's about the difference between faith practiced with structure and faith left to rot. *Powwow* wasn't a danger to anyone. The danger began when its rules were ignored.

*Braucherei*, like any good system of magic, works through order. The job starts with figuring out what you're really facing—something physical, emotional, or spiritual. Only then do you decide which prayer, herb, or verse belongs to it. Every worker knows the steps: cleanse, ground, pray, confirm, act. You don't skip steps, and you don't move out of fear. John Blymire did it backwards. He started with accusation, fed by panic, and called it ritual.

In *powwow*, healing and harm live side by side because the same verse can do either depending on how it's used. The Bible line that stops bleeding can also bind an enemy if it's spoken with anger instead of faith. That's why discernment comes first. You make sure of what's really happening before you open your mouth. Blymire never did. He took bad luck as proof and turned a healer's name into evidence of guilt.

When he went after Rehmeyer's hair and his book, he was following the shape of a real working but without the safeguards. In both German and Appalachian practice, burning a person's taglock with a charm or text tied to them can cut an unhealthy bond. It's done under protection, usually after divination has confirmed the tie is real. You clear the space, pray, speak your intent, and end with cleansing. None of that happened in York County. They skipped straight to destruction.

What they did wasn't a spell. It was fear pretending to be one.

The lesson here reaches past time and place. Every kind of magic, whether it be hoodoo, *powwow*, conjure, or witchcraft, has its guardrails. They aren't decoration or moral window dressing. They're the frame that keeps the work steady and keeps power from folding back on the worker. In the Hollow that night, those guardrails were gone. Fear dressed itself up like ritual, and fear is always leads to bad magic.

Talk to workers now and you'll still hear the same mistake. Somebody comes in saying, "I think I've been cursed. My money's gone. My health's off. Everything's turned against me." Sometimes they're right. Sometimes they're tired, grieving, or dodging responsibility. The first question any good worker asks is simple: *Is this a spirit problem or a life problem?* If you can't tell, you don't start lighting candles and naming enemies. You start with cleansing, rest, and divination. Anything else is just fear pretending to be power.

Rehmeyer's story shows another pattern too—the way people turn suspicion on the ones who help them. The healer who blesses the field gets blamed for the blight. The midwife who eases a birth becomes the witch when a baby dies. It's the same anywhere magic lives close to need. Power that isn't understood always looks dangerous to somebody.

The wise learn to work quietly and keep what they're doing private. Not out of shame, but for their own safety and for the safety of the magic they practice.

For anyone who works this way, this story is a reminder that good intention isn't enough. Magic needs context. A verse without faith is just noise. A ritual without focus is confusion. When people move from fear instead of trust, they don't break curses, they spread them. Power raised in panic doesn't know where to go, and most times it lands right back on the one who sent it.

That's why serious workers keep rules. Not church rules. Working rules. Don't start what you can't clean up. Don't strike at what you haven't studied. Don't destroy what you don't understand. Those rules keep everybody safe whether it is believers, skeptics, and everyone in between.

Nelson Rehmeyer understood that. He kept his work simple: healing, blessing, prayer. He didn't boast. He didn't compete. That quiet way of working is why folks trusted him. But quiet can look dangerous to the frightened. To someone desperate for control, a calm worker looks powerful—maybe too powerful. That same tension still dogs healers now. People want help, but deep down they're scared of what you might be able to do. It's built into this kind of work: the same hands that mend are always imagined to harm.

What killed Nelson Rehmeyer wasn't *powwow*. It was

projection. Blymire took the weight of his own failures and hung it on the man who looked strong enough to carry it. That's an old reflex. When people can't face what's broken in themselves, they find someone solid and call it a curse. Magic gives that fear a shape and teeth. When belief joins with panic, it stops being faith and turns into superstition. And superstition mixed with desperation is deadly.

There's another piece to name here. The working Blymire tried to do of burning hair with a book. This belongs to a family of reversal spells found all over Europe and Africa. When it's done right, it isn't about revenge. It's about release. You cut the tie, cleanse, and move on. You don't burn the person. You burn the link. Without that understanding, what happened in 1928 looks like magic, but it was really fear trying to wear ritual's clothes.

Every place that keeps old magic alive has a story like this—one that warns against acting on guesswork. The Hex Murder is Pennsylvania's version. It shows what happens when belief stops checking itself. Real power asks questions. Real faith tests its own motives. Skip that step and you're not working magic anymore. You're just giving shape to panic.

The duty that comes with this path hasn't changed. If you call yourself a worker, healer, conjure man, or powwow doctor—anyone who stands between the seen and unseen, you owe your people discipline. You owe them honesty. You owe them the promise that you won't turn their fear into fire.

Because every charm, every prayer, every spell carries the echo of whatever built it. Work from peace and peace spreads. Work from fear and fear multiplies. That's the real haunting in York County—the echo of panic turned loose, a thought repeated until it became an act of violence.

And if the story of Nelson Rehmeyer still stirs unease a century later, it's because the lesson is still true. Magic without boundaries becomes harm. Faith without understanding becomes danger. And the cost of both always falls on whoever's standing closest.

## THE SIGNS

The house still stands in York County, set back from the road and half hidden by trees that lean toward each other like they're keeping a secret. The roof's been replaced, the porch rebuilt, but the ground around it hasn't changed. Folks who make the trip all say the same thing first—the air feels heavier there. Not colder. Just dense, like the space between sound and silence has been stretched thin. You don't have to believe in spirits to notice it. You just have to stand still long enough.

People call it Rehmeyer's Hollow now. The name has outlived everyone who ever lived there. Local kids dare each other to drive up after dark. Some turn back before they reach the gate. A few go inside, hoping for proof, and come away quiet. Not shaken. Just thoughtful. The kind of quiet that means something got under their skin.

The stories about the house stay steady. Nobody says they see full figures or hear voices. What they describe instead are small interruptions like watches that stop until they step outside again, phones that lose signal, a smell of burned wood that comes and goes. The kitchen, where the body was found, is said to be the stillest part. Even people who don't know the story slow down when they cross that room. They don't talk about ghosts. They talk about presence.

A woman who grew up nearby told an interviewer her mother used to leave a bowl of milk at the edge of the woods every November. She never called it an offering. She just said it kept the place calm. When asked if she believed Nelson Rehmeyer's spirit was still there, she shrugged and said, "Something is." That's how real folk belief survives—quietly, without need for proof. You don't argue what's real. You just do what keeps the balance.

Neighbors tell another story, quieter still. After the murder, some claimed they'd seen Rehmeyer walking the edge of his land at dusk. Not a glowing ghost, just a man moving through his own field, shoulders bent, not turning his head. Maybe it was imagination. Maybe it was grief. Either way, no one called out.

They just nodded toward the trees and kept their distance.

There's an uneasiness that never left those hills. It isn't the haunting of one man. It's the echo of a community that saw belief turn to violence and didn't know how to speak of it after. For years, *powwow* workers kept their practice quiet. It was not because they were doing harm, but because they didn't want to be blamed for it. The silence became its own ghost, passed from family to family, a warning carried by memory instead of story.

Every so often somebody tries to explain the house's reputation with science blaming magnetic fields, carbon monoxide, or the power of suggestion. Maybe some of that's true. But places remember emotion the same way people do. The floorboards in that kitchen have soaked up a hundred years of retelling. Every visitor adds another layer of attention, and attention is its own kind of energy. When enough people look at a place with equal parts fear and fascination, the air starts to hold it. That's the haunting most of us know. Not a ghost, just a feeling that won't lift until the truth comes out.

Old Pennsylvania lore warns against stirring ground that's seen unbalanced magic. "What was done in anger stays in the soil," the saying goes, "until someone prays with understanding." That's the reason behind the small things people still do without calling them ritual. A handful of salt scattered on the step after a funeral. A quiet prayer before driving into the Hollow. A candle lit when the date comes around. Those acts don't erase what happened. They steady it.

The danger that lingers in those hills isn't a vengeful spirit. It's the idea that harm always wears a human face you can punish. That's the same thinking that killed Nelson Rehmeyer. It moves quieter now, but it's still here every time someone points at a neighbor and says, "They're the reason things keep going wrong." That kind of talk is its own curse. It spreads by word instead of spell, and it doesn't need ritual to do damage.

People who stay long enough to sit in the Hollow after dark describe a kind of surrender. The wind moves through the bare trees, making a sound low and steady, like a hum under the breath. It isn't frightening. It's tired. The land isn't angry. It's just worn out from being misunderstood. Most folks leave slower than they came. Some stop by the roadside cross on the way out and drop a coin, just in case. Nobody tells them to. They just feel like it's the right thing to do.

In folklore, when a story settles so deep in a place that it starts changing how people act, that's called a living haunting. Rehmeyer's Hollow fits the rule. The fear that once caused a killing now keeps people cautious and polite toward what they can't explain. Maybe that's the land's way of balancing itself by turning a lesson into a warning, turning violence into quiet.

Whatever else may walk there, it isn't vengeance. It's memory. And memory, when left alone too long, starts to sound like footsteps coming down an empty road.

## THE WORK

The Hex Murder of York County wasn't sorcery gone wrong. It was people skipping the steps that keep power clean. What happened in that farmhouse is what happens any time belief runs faster than discipline. A man died not because his work was dark, but because someone mistook fear for proof. The cure for that kind of confusion hasn't changed. It's reflection, cleansing, and restraint.

Anyone who works with magic, prayer, or energy carries two duties. The first is to know your own condition before you start. The second is to keep other people's fear from feeding the work. Forget either one and the power starts to twist. That's why most traditions teach the same order: cleanse first, question second, act last. You can't see straight through a spirit that's clouded by panic.

The story in York County reminds us that protection magic isn't just for spirits or curses. It's for human impulse—the urge to blame, the rush to fix. The work that follows here is meant to clear confusion and hold integrity, not strike. It brings power back to balance.

When something in your life feels off—illness, worry, a run of bad luck, you start by washing it off yourself, not by naming an enemy. Fill a bowl with clean water. Add a pinch of salt and a sprig of hyssop or rosemary if you have it. Sit with the bowl until the water goes still. Look into it and say, slow and plain: *"If this heaviness is mine, let it rise and dissolve. If it belongs elsewhere, let it go back in peace."*

Dip your fingers in the water and touch your forehead, the palms of your hands, and the soles of your feet. These are the gates where power enters and leaves the body. When you're done, pour the water outside, never down a drain. You're not throwing it away; you're giving the earth permission to clear it. Do this for three nights while the moon wanes. That rhythm matches release, not retaliation.

If the heaviness runs deeper, such as something that's been sitting on you for years, write your name on brown paper and fold it toward you once. Slide it under a small bowl of salted water and light a black candle beside it. The candle stands for focus, not darkness. Let it burn itself out while you pray or just breathe. When it's done, bury the paper and pour the water into the soil.

For those who work in the open—readers, charm-workers, *powwow* healers, spiritual counselors—protection of your craft has to include reputation.

Misunderstanding is its own kind of harm. To keep the air around your name steady, make a small charm that sends truth back where it belongs.

Take a pocket-sized mirror and wipe it with a damp cloth sprinkled with salt. Say your name out loud and speak: *"Let what is mine be seen clearly. Let what is not mine pass through."* Wrap the mirror in black cloth and tie it with red thread in three knots. Keep it near the door where clients or guests enter, or on the altar where you pray. Once a month, unwrap it, breathe on the glass, and repeat your words. That's spiritual maintenance, not ceremony. You're reminding the world who you are and what you're not.

If false talk starts moving around your name, don't answer it with argument. Hold the wrapped mirror for a moment, say your name again, and set it under your pillow for one night. In the morning, put it back in its place. The charm doesn't fight gossip. It releases its grip.

Folk magic runs on reciprocity. What you send out meets you on its way back. The quickest way to curse yourself is to treat fear like proof. Before you work a reversal or a binding, ask three questions. Have I cleansed myself first? Have I sought divination or counsel? Am I acting from peace or from panic? If any answer leans toward panic, stop. Go back to cleansing. The world won't end while you wait for clarity.

Rehmeyer's story stands as the reminder. Belief stays neutral until it moves. Once you act, power takes shape, and shape has consequence. The verse, the flame, the spoken charm—each one amplifies whatever spirit you're already in. That's why humility is the strongest shield in any kind of work. It keeps the hands steady and the ego quiet.

If the weight of accusation ever falls on you, if people decide your craft must be the reason their luck soured, don't argue belief with them. Protect your spirit. Keep your words measured. Say your prayer. Let the proof of your life speak for itself.

The difference between *powwow* and the panic that killed a man in 1928 is the difference between discipline and fear. Real magic heals by bringing things back into order. False magic harms by acting without it. The first begins with stillness. The second begins with blame.

That's the lesson written into the floorboards of that farmhouse: cleanse before you accuse, pray before you act, tell the truth before you light the fire.

Because in every system that works with power, the rule never changes. What you send out finds its way home.

## ABOUT THE LONG LOST FRIEND

In Pennsylvania Dutch country, nearly every farmhouse once kept a small book near the Bible. It was called *The Long Lost Friend*, and it promised protection, healing, and safety for anyone who owned it. The verses inside weren't spells in the dramatic sense. They were prayers, charms, and folk remedies collected by John George Hohman in the early 1800s. He wrote them in both German and English so that immigrants could carry their traditions into the new world without leaving their faith behind.

Each page blended scripture with practicality. "To stop bleeding, recite this verse." "To protect your cattle, hang this charm." It was Christianity written in the language of daily survival. For families who lived far from doctors or ministers, that book was a safeguard—proof that belief could work with its hands. Farmers carried copies in coat pockets. Mothers read them over fevers. A worker who owned *The Long Lost Friend* was thought to be under God's special care, as long as the text was respected.

The truth is simple. *The Long Lost Friend* was never a dark manual. It was a record of how ordinary people met hardship with prayer and intention. The danger wasn't in the words. It was in forgetting the discipline behind them. Books don't hex. People do, when fear replaces understanding and logic.

# THE TOMB OF MARIE LAVEAU

The ground inside St. Louis Cemetery No. 1 never lies flat. The brick paths buckle where tree roots have pushed from below, and the gravel shifts with every step. The air tastes of stone, salt, and the faint sweetness of flowers that dried weeks ago. The tombs stand close together, whitewashed and cracked, their edges bleeding rust from the old iron that holds them upright. Nothing here feels finished.

If you stay long enough, you start to notice the layers of sound. A church bell somewhere off in the distance. A streetcar a few blocks away. The shuffle of shoes from a tour group moving down another row. But closer, inside this small city of the dead, there's another kind of noise—the hush that settles when too many prayers have been spoken in the same square of air. It isn't silence. It's density. The weight of every voice that came before.

One tomb draws more visitors than all the rest. It isn't large. It isn't ornate. Its plastered surface is stained with weather and with offerings that melted into the paint. Coins rest in the cracks. Red wax has hardened into thin rivers. And everywhere you look are the same marks: three X's, carved, scratched, or drawn in whatever someone had on hand. Some are bright, some faded, some half-erased by caretakers who paint over them again and again.

People come for reasons that never sound the same when spoken but rise from the same need. Some ask for healing. Some for love. Some for justice they can't find among the living. A few stand silent, too respectful or too unsure to speak. Most leave something behind like a candle, a coin, a lock of hair tied with ribbon, or a folded note pressed so tight it looks like a seed.

The tomb belongs to Marie Catherine Laveau, buried here in 1881 yet never gone from the city she helped shape. Folks in New Orleans will tell you plain that she still works. They mean it. Whatever you believe, the proof stands right in front of you in the heat, in the marks, and in the steady line of hands that reach for her stone.

## THE HISTORY

Marie Laveau lives in a space half fact, half legend, and the line between them has never been clear. Newspapers of her day called her a sorceress, a queen of voodoo, a dangerous woman who held the city in her spell. Painters and storytellers turned her into myth and describe her as barefoot in white linen, a snake across her shoulders, eyes that could call down storms. The truth is quieter, and stronger.

She was born in 1801, a free woman of color in a city where freedom and bondage, privilege and danger, lived side by side. Her mother, Marguerite, was of African and Native descent. Her father, Charles Laveau, carried French blood and local standing. Marie grew up in the Creole quarter, where French, Spanish, African, and Caribbean traditions met and mingled until nobody could tell where one ended and another began. She was baptized Catholic and stayed devout, but she also learned that religion and ritual could share the same altar.

As a young woman she married Jacques Paris, a Haitian man who disappeared a few years after the wedding. Some said he died. Others said he went back to the islands. Either way, Marie was left alone. She supported herself as a hairdresser, a job that placed her in the parlors of wealthy white women who treated gossip like gold. She listened. She remembered. And she built quiet lines of information that would one day make her indispensable.

By the 1820s she had formed a romantic bond with Louis Glapion, a carpenter of mixed heritage. They never married in the church, but they lived as husband and wife for decades and raised several children. Some died young. Others may have carried on her work. The record blurs because the lives of free people of color were rarely written down with care.

By the 1830s, Marie Laveau's name carried weight all over New Orleans. She was known as a faithful Catholic, a regular at Mass, and active in charity work. But she was also known as a *voudou mambo*, a priestess who spoke with spirits and ancestors. The practice she led was Louisiana Voudou, a blend of West African belief, Native medicine, and Catholic devotion. It worked through prayer, herbs, drumming, dance, and offerings that kept balance between the living and the dead.

She held public ceremonies in Congo Square, the open ground where enslaved Africans once gathered on Sundays. Under the sound of drums and the eyes of both believers and onlookers, she led rituals of thanks and release. The authorities alternated between tolerance and fear, depending on who held office that year. What made her powerful wasn't display. It was results. People saw her work, and knew that it worked.

Her house on St. Ann Street was part clinic, part chapel, part counseling room. Those who could pay left coins or gifts. Those who couldn't left prayers. She mixed herbs for fever, blessed charms for travel, made *gris-gris* for protection, and prayed over the sick. Her name passed through every corner of the city from the poorest Black families to judges, politicians, and Creoles who visited her at night so the neighbors wouldn't talk.

Marie Laveau's influence crossed every line the city tried to draw. White citizens feared her and still sought her help. Black and Creole residents called her leader and protector. The newspapers never knew what to make of her. One week she was a saint, the next a witch, then a healer, then a criminal. What they couldn't bring themselves to print was the truth: she was a powerful black woman and beyond their control.

When Marie Laveau died in 1881, the obituary writers tried to shrink her back to human size. They called her "the celebrated colored woman" and noted, with careful respect, that her funeral at St. Louis Cathedral was well attended. But within months people were saying she was still walking the streets. Some claimed to see her kneeling in the pews again. Others swore they met her by the river at dusk. Whether it was her daughter (also named Marie) or the spirit of the same woman hardly mattered. New Orleans accepted both.

Her resting place, the Glapion family tomb in St. Louis Cemetery No. 1, became a site of pilgrimage almost right away. Folks who had gone to her in life now came to her in death. They left small gifts and whispered their wishes. By the turn of the century, visitors were marking her tomb with three X's, turning in circles, knocking on the plaster, and promising to come back with thanks if their prayers were answered. Nobody knows when that started or why the sign caught on. It isn't part of classical Voudou, but folk magic follows its own sense. An X marks a crossroads, and three repeats fix the intention. The pattern made sense to the people who needed it to.

Over time the tomb gathered layers of belief. Tourists came, then spiritual seekers, then the simply curious. The Archdiocese painted and patched it again and again, each coat hiding hundreds of marks that always returned. The rules changed to licensed tours only with limited access but it didn't limit devotion. People still press coins into the mortar, still leave rum and flowers at the gate when they can't get inside.

What they're really doing, whether they know it or not, is keeping up a conversation with the dead. In Afro-Creole tradition, the departed aren't silent. They listen. They answer. The line between grave and altar grows thin when enough faith gathers in one place. Marie Laveau's tomb crossed that line a long time ago.

Each offering adds to the current, a charge built from a century of hope, fear, and thanks. Every petition strengthens the next. Over time the energy of belief reshapes the ground itself. It stops being a memorial and becomes a working, a living meeting place between the living and the unseen.

More than 140 years after her burial, Marie Laveau remains one of the most active spirits in American folk tradition. Her legend travels in songs and guidebooks, but her presence stays local, tied to that humid patch of earth. She reminds us that not all saints are canonized, not all magic hides indoors, and not every grave knows how to stay quiet.

## THE MAGIC

What happens at Marie Laveau's tomb is more than tourism. Every act that happens there—the coins, the marks, the whispered names—is a spell, whether or not the person doing it knows the language. The power that gathers in that spot works like any other spell: intention spoken, spirit acknowledged, exchange made. The only difference is that this one never stops.

In folk practice the dead aren't gone. They're power that's changed form. When you stand at a grave and speak aloud, you're talking into a current that can answer. Marie Laveau's tomb shows what happens when that magical current keeps being fed for over a hundred years. The offerings left there—candles, rum, flowers, jewelry, lipstick, and folded notes speak their own language. Each one says something different: *I'm asking. I'm thankful. I'm paying. I'm coming back.* The tomb receives them the same way a living altar would, taking them in until the air itself starts to hum.

A place like that becomes what rootworkers call *hot ground.* Hot doesn't mean dangerous. It means active. It's a place that knows how to move power when it's called. Every visitor who comes with true need adds to it. Every answered prayer strengthens it. The more people believe, the more the place remembers.

That's why so many who visit feel a weight in the chest or warmth in the hands. They've stepped onto charged ground. The tomb holds what's been given to it for generations: faith, fear, longing, gratitude. Every offering teaches the place what to do with that power, and after this long, it knows.

The ritual of the three X's tells the story on its own. The X is an old mark of crossing and contact, the meeting point of two lines—one from above, one from below. In crossroads work it stands for choice and for agreement. When three X's appear together, the meaning builds: petition, confirmation, completion. The knocking that follows is a signal that the visitor has arrived. Turning three times seals the act, lining up body, mind, and spirit in one motion. Nobody has to teach these gestures. They're older than the names people give them. Folk magic always builds its own grammar.

People sometimes ask if the spirit that answers is truly Marie Laveau or a collective force that carries her name. From a worker's view, it doesn't much matter. Power moves where attention goes. When thousands of people focus their faith on one image, that focus shapes a presence that can respond. Some might call it an egregore. In Voudou it's a spirit raised through devotion. In hoodoo it's an ancestor who never quit working. The name changes. The result stays the same.

The way she answers follows the same law as any other kind of magic. You bring what you have to give whether it's a coin, a candle, a kind word and you receive back what balance allows. Some wishes come through clear. Others shift things so slowly you only see it after. Not every "no" is refusal. Sometimes it's protection. Spirits that move at her level don't hand out luck; they correct flow.

That's why return is part of the deal. Every working with the dead needs closure. When somebody's wish is granted and they don't go back to give thanks, the work stays open. Energy that's left open goes looking for balance, often by finding the one who started it. That's where the stories around her tomb come from—people who forgot to repay and watched their lives start to fray in small, stubborn ways. It isn't punishment. It's simple cause and effect in spiritual form. You close the circle to keep the peace.

Offerings at Marie Laveau's tomb show who still calls on her. Hair ties and lipstick come from women asking for strength, beauty, or courage. Coins speak of thanks and payment. Rum and perfume belong to the language of respect and celebration—signs that the visitor knows Creole custom. Written petitions are the clearest talk of all, ink turned into intention. When all of these gather at once, the tomb becomes a living record of what people need.

For modern workers, that matters because it shows how magic stays alive. The acts at her grave aren't copies of nineteenth-century Voudou. They've changed with time, but they still hold the same frame of exchange. Every real spell rests on three things: acknowledgment of spirit, offering of exchange, and acceptance of outcome. The visitors who follow those steps, even by instinct, keep the current moving.

Her power came from a specific root of African, Catholic, Creole, and female in a world that fought all four. To stand at her tomb without honoring that mix is to miss the point. You can honor her as ancestor, healer, or saint, but you do it with humility. You don't demand. You don't mimic what you don't understand. You recognize the history that made her. That respect is part of the offering.

People often ask if it's safe for outsiders to work there. The answer depends on approach. Magic listens to sincerity more than lineage, but arrogance burns fast. If you go to a spirit for help, you go willing to listen. The rules are the same as visiting a living elder: announce yourself, speak plain, give thanks, and leave quiet.

From a worker's view, her tomb stands as a threshold. It holds the balance of earth, because it's grave ground; fire, from the candles; and water, from the air that never dries. Those three together make a place where change comes easier. That's why prayers spoken there often find quick footing. The air itself helps the work.

The lasting strength of that place proves another truth—that magic is community work. One person may start a ritual, but only shared faith keeps it alive after death. Thousands of small gestures have fed the power around that tomb. Each visit renews the bond between the living and the dead. That's how a ritual turns into heritage.

Marie Laveau's tomb reminds every worker that

power doesn't end when life does. It moves. It becomes part of the air. You can feel it in the warmth of the stone, in the weight of the air, in the knowing that something is listening. The wise meet that attention with respect, not fear. Because once a spirit proves steady, it isn't haunting anymore. It's helping.

## THE SIGNS

The cemeteries of New Orleans don't pretend to be quiet. The heat keeps the air moving, and the traffic of the living never stops. Yet around Marie Laveau's tomb there's a stillness that doesn't belong to weather or time. It isn't eerie in the storybook sense. It feels deliberate, as if the place itself is listening. Guides who walk those paths every day say sound behaves differently there. Words seem to land heavy around there like they're stuck in the air.

Visitors talk about things that can't be blamed on suggestion like fthe sudden smell of tobacco or rosewater, a pressure in the air that feels like a hand on the shoulder, the sense that someone is standing just outside your sight. The most common report isn't fear. It's attention. That feeling of being noticed by something that weighs your intent before deciding whether to answer. People who come expecting chills often leave calm, as if a question has been heard even without a reply.

Stories circle about a woman seen near the Glapion tomb after hours. Some call her the woman in white, others the woman in red. Always barefoot. Always walking with purpose. She moves through the crypts like she's inspecting them, pauses at Marie's grave, then disappears behind a wall with no doorway. A maintenance worker once said she left footprints in the dry dust even though it hadn't rained in weeks. He swept them away before sunrise and found them again the next morning.

One evening a tour guide stayed behind after her group left, collecting candles that had burned down to glass puddles. She looked up and saw a figure in the next aisle—tall, still, dressed in a faded skirt. Thinking it was another visitor lingering, she offered to walk her out. The woman nodded but said nothing. When the guide turned the corner, the path was empty. What hung in the air was a thin scent of tobacco, roses, and something metallic, like the air before rain. She kept that story to herself for years, not out of fear, but because she didn't want it to sound like she was trading on a private moment.

Other stories are quieter. A candle that lights without flame. Coins that shift from one corner of the tomb to another. Wax that melts into shapes that look like letters. A young man once said his candle flared to life while he was still setting his petition paper. He took it as a sign that she'd heard him and walked away fast— half afraid, half thankful. The next week his court case settled in his favor. He came back with rum and flowers, cleaned the space, and left without a word.

The caretakers still mention him because he was one of the few who returned twice.

Among the local guides there are customs that never made it into any rule book. Some carry a silver coin on every tour, a quiet payment if they speak too freely about the Queen's life. Others won't say her name while facing the tomb. They turn slightly away, telling her story instead of speaking to her. It isn't fear. It's manners. Words are offerings too and getting them right is part of the respect.

Even the skeptics leave changed. One journalist wrote that she expected the tomb to feel theatrical like a stage for superstition. Instead, she said, it felt heavy. The air pressed down like humidity thick with history. She left a quarter on the ledge without meaning to, only noticing it when she stepped through the gate. She didn't go back for it. Most people don't.

Every city with deep roots has a place like this—a point where story and presence meet until they can't be separated. In New Orleans, that place is here. The marks on the plaster aren't vandalism. They're continuity. Every scratch, every coin, every whispered thank-you is part of a ritual that keeps the boundary between worlds open and at ease. The power in this tomb isn't menace. It's maintenance.

But there are cautions whispered by the people who live nearby. One caretaker said he can tell when someone has broken a promise to Marie because the air around the tomb feels wrong—fa kind of charge, like the moment before lightning. Within days a visitor usually returns, cleaning, replacing, finishing what they left undone. Coincidence or balance, no one argues it anymore. The pattern shows itself too often. You don't ask unless you plan to repay.

That rule reaches past this one grave. It mirrors the law that runs through the whole city. New Orleans lives on exchange between land and water, past and present, saints and spirits. Marie Laveau's tomb just makes that rule visible. Stand there at dusk, when the light turns the white tombs gold and the air smells of rum and wax, and you'll understand why no one calls it haunted. The word doesn't fit. The place isn't held by a restless dead. It's tended by an active one.

People leave the cemetery quietly, stepping back into the noise of the Quarter with the same care they'd use walking out of a church. They might laugh once the gate shuts behind them, shake off the weight, or stop for coffee close by. But almost all of them, whether they admit it or not, look back once before they turn the corner. Not from fear. From respect. In New Orleans, the polite thing is to say goodbye.

## THE WORK

Marie Laveau's tomb isn't famous because of its legend. It is because people keep showing up as if she's still listening. Every whisper, every mark, every offering has worked itself into that stone until the line between grave and altar is gone. What's left is a living exchange—the living speak, the spirit answers, and the work keeps moving.

The lesson isn't about spectacle. It's about relationship. What happens at that tomb shows how folk magic survives: through respect, repetition, and follow-through. Everyone who comes adds another thread to a pattern that started with gratitude and obligation. When a wish is granted, you close the circle by giving thanks. It's called manners.

For anyone who steps onto sacred ground, the same rules hold no matter where you are. A cemetery isn't a stage for proof; it's a crossing place. Treat it like a door and it'll act like one. Knock with respect, speak plain, and leave it better than you found it.

If you ever ask for help at a grave, Marie's or anyone's, begin with simple acknowledgment. You're not commanding the dead; you're consulting them. Bring three simple things: a coin, a candle, and a small drink of water or rum. The coin is payment. The candle offers light. The water refreshes. Set them at the base of the marker and stand still until the air settles. Then say your name and speak what you need. Talk like you're asking an elder for advice.

When you finish, thank the spirit and step back three paces before you turn away. Don't speak again until you've crossed the gate. That quiet moment is part of sealing the work. If help comes, if the job appears, the pain eases, or the outcome bends your way, then you return. Bring a second offering. Wipe the stone clean. Say thank you out loud. These aren't superstitions. They're manners. The same as closing a door you've opened.

If nothing happens, let it rest. Some spirits say no to protect you. Others just aren't tied to your path. Either way, gratitude is still owed for being heard. You don't ask the dead for proof. You take responsibility for your own next step.

Sometimes people visit a grave not to ask a favor, but to pay a debt, to thank a spirit, or to release old emotion. Write on a small piece of brown paper: *Thank you for the help I received. I return all debts paid in peace.* Fold the paper toward you once, set it under a white candle, and light the wick. While it burns, pour a little water or rum at the foot of the grave and speak the same words aloud. When the candle's gone out, bury the cooled wax nearby or take it with you to drop in moving water. That gesture clears the connection but keeps the respect.

Working with the dead, especially someone like Marie Laveau, requires awareness. She was a free woman of color who held authority. To stand at her tomb without remembering that history is to take the work out of context. You don't have to claim her lineage to honor it, but you do have to remember whose ground you're standing on. Recognizing the culture that shaped her is part of the offering.

In folk magic, intention and posture decide the outcome. Arrogance shuts doors. Humility opens them. When you step into a cemetery, you're not in neutral ground. You're walking through all the memories of those who are there and those who loved them. Treat it like any household that's invited you in: speak softly, don't take what isn't yours, and leave something in thanks.

Every prayer whispered at Marie Laveau's tomb adds to its power. Over the years those prayers have turned faith into structure. The place hums because of consistency.

If you go there, listen before you speak. Pay before you ask. Keep your word when you leave. That respect is what keeps the magic clean.

Marie Laveau's tomb isn't famous because of superstition. It's about the power that continues to happen there because it is fed by its visitors. That's what makes a place sacred: steady exchange between those who need and those who can answer.

When you walk away from her gate, the air will feel different. That's how you know you've been heard. Offer a quiet thank-you to the wind, and don't look back. The conversation isn't finished. It's waiting for the next person who understands that asking is easy, but gratitude is the real magic.

# ELIZABETH BATHORY-
# THE BLOOD COUNTESS

The wind moves differently through ruins. It doesn't travel straight across the ground the way it does through open fields. It circles, tracing the shape of what used to stand. At Cachtice Castle, that wind carries centuries of dust and rumor. The roof is gone, the windows long since fallen in, and the walls rise just high enough to remind you of what's missing. Step inside and the silence doesn't feel empty, it feels restrained, like the air has learned to hold its breath.

The hills below are still green, dotted with farms that look ordinary until you realize how long the valley has been watching this ridge. From a distance, the ruin seems harmless, a pale line of stone against the sky. Up close, the light shifts. It dulls, as if the castle absorbs it. The space feels balanced between memory and judgment, and even those who swear they don't believe in hauntings lower their voices once they step past what used to be the threshold.

This is where Elizabeth Bathory lived, ruled, and died. To some she's a monster. To others she's a warning about what happens when a woman refuses to obey. Her story still rides the wind in this place. The details change from one telling to the next, but the shape is the same: young women disappeared, accusations grew, a door was sealed from the outside, and a name stopped belonging to a person and became a symbol. That part, at least, is true.

Cachtice Castle is ruin now, but the story built here still stands. It isn't a ghost story, and it isn't clean history either. It lives in the space between, where evidence and superstition overlap.

## THE HISTORY

Elizabeth Bathory—Erzsébet Báthory in her own tongue—was born in 1560 into one of the most powerful families in Hungary. The Báthory name carried prestige across the region. Her relatives had been bishops, princes, and military leaders. Their alliances reached into royal courts. Her parents were cousins, married to keep property and titles inside the family—a common practice among nobles who treated marriage as business, not affection. The result was a bloodline that mixed power with instability: educated, insular, and fiercely protective of its own authority.

Her childhood reflected that ambition. She received an education rare even for noblemen. She spoke Hungarian, Latin, German, and Greek. She studied law, philosophy, and mathematics. Her tutors wrote that she had a sharp, questioning mind, that she wanted to know *why*, not just *what*. That alone was enough to make people uneasy. In sixteenth-century Hungary, obedience was valued in daughters far more than intellect.

At fifteen she married Ferenc Nádasdy, heir to another great house. The match served both families. Her inheritance brought money; his military career brought favor. Their estates stretched across the Carpathians, and among the properties exchanged was Cachtice Castle. It was a fortress meant to guard trade routes and, eventually, the place that would guard her story.

Ferenc spent most of his years fighting the Ottomans, leaving Elizabeth to run their holdings. The records that remain show she did it well. She settled disputes, kept detailed accounts, and acted as her husband's proxy in legal matters. That might sound practical now, but then it was radical. A woman running land and people on her own didn't sit right with men who thought power should stay in their hands.

The first stories of cruelty began during those years she spent alone. Servants whispered about punishments that went too far. Some said Ferenc, hardened by war, had taught her his own ways of discipline. He would put paper soaked in oil between a servant's toes and set on it fire, or smeared their bodies with honey and left them out for the insects. Nobody can prove it ever happened. But rumor has always been the poor man's weapon. When you can't face power directly, you tell stories about it until the truth starts to show through.

When Ferenc died in 1604, Elizabeth didn't remarry. She inherited everything: his lands, his wealth, his staff, and ruled them herself. That freedom quickly turned against her. A woman of rank who refused to be managed unsettled everyone who expected her to obey. Each sickness, each disappearance on her estates began to look like proof of sin. Hungary was already raw from plague, famine, and war, and people wanted someone to blame. Elizabeth was visible, and visibility has never been safe for a woman who doesn't apologize for being her own person.

The first reports spoke of missing maids. Then came rumors of noble daughters sent to her court for refinement who came back sick, or never came back at all. In a world where reputation was currency, every story damaged the families tied to her. They passed those tales along louder each time, maybe to clear themselves of scandal. What started as accusation spread like infection.

By 1610 the crown took notice, mostly because the timing suited it. King Matthias II owed the Báthorys a debt so heavy it could have broken the treasury. But if Elizabeth were found guilty of crimes against the realm, her estates could be seized and her accounts absorbed. It was an elegant solution—financial relief dressed up as moral outrage.

The investigation fell to György Thurzó, the Palatine of Hungary and Elizabeth's cousin. His duty pulled both ways: loyalty to family and loyalty to crown. The easiest path was to seem impartial while guiding the verdict where it needed to land. He gathered testimony from servants and villagers, some willing, many broken under torture. The numbers grew with every retelling. Thirty victims became a hundred, then three hundred, and by the time the scribes were done, the count had climbed to six hundred fifty. Somewhere in those papers appeared a rumor of a diary that listed every name, though no such book ever surfaced.

When Thurzó's men raided the castle that winter, they said they found bodies and others dying from wounds. The descriptions read like theatrical script with details arranged to shock, not to record. The servants were tried and executed almost at once. One had her fingers torn off before being burned. Another was ripped with hot pincers. A third was beaten to death in public.

Elizabeth never saw a trial. Executing a countess would have split the nobility but locking her away quietly served everyone's interest.

They sealed her inside her own home. Workers bricked the windows and left only a small slot in the door for food. The plan was to erase her slowly, giving the world time to forget. She lived four more years in that cell. Guards said they heard prayers at night, then nothing.

When she died in 1614, villagers refused her burial. Her body was moved in secret—far enough away that the church could declare peace restored, though nothing about her story was ever completely settled.

The detail that made Elizabeth Bathory immortal, the blood baths, didn't appear until nearly a century later.

None of the original testimonies mention them. That part came from pamphlet writers who knew a story of torture might fade away, but a story of a woman bathing in blood would live forever. By the nineteenth century, gothic authors had turned her into Europe's female vampire, changing accusation into art and superstition into big business.

Behind the invention sits a plainer truth. Young women did die at Cachtice. Some were servants, some apprentices, some daughters of small nobles. Whether they died from cruelty or from neglect, we can't know. What history recorded wasn't justice—it was convenience. The church gained leverage. The crown settled its debt. And the legend of Elizabeth Bathory gave Europe one of its favorite pictures of a dangerous woman.

The story stays alive because it still intrigues. It warns that intelligence turns to arrogance when it belongs to a woman, that discipline turns to cruelty when a woman enforces it, and that solitude turns to sin when a woman chooses it. The accusation only had to sound true once. After that, it carried itself.

Cachtice Castle still stands on its hill, stripped of walls but not of meaning. Each fallen stone shows another layer of how fear builds itself into a place. People go there looking for ghosts and find something heavier—the proof that a story built on punishment can outlast every reason it was told.

## THE MAGIC

Every lasting legend serves a purpose. Some warn. Some excuse. Some hold a mirror to what a culture fears most. The story of Elizabeth Bathory endures because it joined three of the oldest symbols people know by instinct—blood, beauty, and control. Whether she killed dozens of girls or none at all, the image built around her became its own ritual: a story teaching that when a woman reaches for power, the world will find a way to call it corruption.

In magic, blood is never decoration. It's the body's signature and the spirit's contract. Across every kind of folk work it's the material that binds. A drop in a charm seals it to its maker. A smear on paper marks ownership. In hoodoo, a woman's menstrual blood mixed into food ties loyalty. In European witchcraft, a pinprick seals secrecy. In African and Caribbean rites, blood offered to the spirits returns strength to balance. It's never casual. It means the worker has chosen to give something that can't be replaced.

When later storytellers said Elizabeth Bathory bathed in the blood of virgins, they reversed everything blood means in real practice. In magic, bathing is cleansing. You mix herbs, salt, or milk to wash away grief, sickness, or crossed conditions. You use water to carry heaviness back into the ground. To bathe in blood turns that on its head. It takes what should cleanse and makes it consume. It changes release into hunger. That's why the image still unsettles people. It isn't just the violence—it's that the ritual itself has been turned inside out.

Then comes the mirror. Every version of her story includes it: a woman watching her own reflection, terrified of time, measuring her worth in glass. In any kind of folk magic, mirrors aren't neutral. They hold onto energy the way water holds a reflection. They're used for scrying, for summoning, for defense. In many homes they're covered when someone dies, so the soul doesn't get caught on the way out. A mirror can tell truth, but it can also feed obsession. In Bathory's legend the mirror becomes her judge, showing her the aging she can't stop. It reminds you of the wicked queen in the tale of Snow White. When a tool for knowledge turns into the instrument of madness, the real lesson appears about beauty becoming a form of power.

Bathory's imprisonment fits the same pattern found in magic. Her sentence wasn't death. It was containment. Folk workers know that when a force can't be cleansed, you bind it. Curses are buried in jars. Spirits that won't leave are sealed in bottles with wax and salt. The nobles of Hungary did the same thing to a living woman. They turned the castle into a working of banishment, bricking her inside to neutralize what they feared. It was politics disguised as exorcism. She wasn't punished only for cruelty but for living beyond their control. The method, closing her off from sight, mirrors how societies treat power they don't understand.

Centuries later, her name works like a sigil. A sigil gains strength through repetition. The more it's drawn or spoken, the more it shapes what it represents. "The Blood Countess" is one of those symbols. Every story, painting, and song that borrows her image adds another charge. She's become an collective energy built from fascination and blame— an example of everything people project onto powerful women: beauty, cruelty, independence, defiance. When modern occultists reach for her, they rarely meet the person. They meet the spirit built from four centuries of attention.

Working with that current means handling raw myth, not a ghost. It answers to focus, not to faith. Practitioners who understand the risk study it more than they summon it, because calling an egregore invites every emotion that formed it. You're not speaking to one presence; you're stepping into generations of fear, desire, and misunderstanding that have gathered around her name.

From a magical view, Bathory's story teaches more about binding than indulgence. It shows what happens when a tale becomes a spell cast by society itself. A community decided she was unclean, repeated it until the idea hardened into truth, and then sealed her away. That's collective intention and it's the same power used in group prayer or protection work, turned instead toward punishment. You might also say it is the same energy used in creating propaganda.

For modern readers, the story also shows how beauty magic and glamour get misunderstood. Real glamour in folk work isn't trickery. It's presentation, deciding what energy to send out so the world meets you on your own terms. Bathory's legend twists that into vanity and hunger, a warning that any woman who uses appearance as power must be taking it from someone else. The story endures because that charge still sticks.

In the end, her legend works like a mirror spell cast on the culture itself. Each retelling reflects what people fear losing most—youth, control, admiration, and what they still think should be punished when it shows up in the wrong hands. The castle may be quiet, but the story keeps going every time her name is spoken. Her tale has become a standing ritual of judgment, showing that proof no longer matters.

## THE SIGNS

Cachtice Castle sits heavy on the hill. The road that climbs toward it is narrow and rough, bordered by trees that close in as you go. From a distance it looks harmless, another monument waiting for photographs. But the closer you walk, the heavier the air feels. The stones give off a dull cold that has nothing to do with the season. Even in summer the place feels half frozen, like time itself was sealed in with whatever was left of her.

There are no whole rooms. The walls stand as outlines with doors that go nowhere and corridors that stop short. Tourists come in daylight, take their pictures, and leave quickly. The guides keep to the facts: architecture, politics, raids, wars. When someone asks about the countess, they lower their voices and give the short version about the accusations, confinement, death. They don't linger. The stories are for the climb up, not the walk down.

Locals say the castle isn't haunted in the usual way. There are no ghosts, no screams, no cold hands reaching from the dark. The haunting lives in the air itself, in the way sound moves when there's nothing to carry it. The wind slips through the gaps like breath caught in a chest. It makes no words, but its rhythm feels deliberate, as if the place has learned to speak without language. Villagers say it "remembers loudly." They don't mean spirits. They mean memory that has turned in something almost tangible.

Among modern workers, her name still rises often enough to prove the land hasn't gone quiet. Practitioners speak of the castle as a focus point—a charged site. They believe it holds power because so many have poured their fear and fascination into it. Each visitor leaves a trace that the stone holds onto. Over time, that buildup behaves like a spell left open too long. It hums. It draws. It bends intention. That's why careful workers come here with respect, not curiosity.

Now and then, stories surface about groups who try calling her name on purpose. The details change, but the pattern stays the same. A handful of people gather at night with red candles, mirrors, and wine meant to stand for blood. They rebuild the legend as ritual with four walls marked with salt, a circle drawn in ash, one name repeated until the air feels thick. The first signs are small. The mirrors fog. The candles pull inward. A scent like metal drifts through the room. Then the air changes. Strange dreams follow. Reflections move when they shouldn't. A pressure builds behind the eyes that makes even ordinary things feel tilted. Some say they called her and she came. Others say they only felt the energy coming from the telling of the story itself.

Folklorists who visit Cachtice talk about a different haunting, one made of story instead of spirit. They come with notebooks and doubt, read the records, measure the facts, and still the place unsettles them. Standing where history and invention are woven so tight changes how memory feels. You can't tell what really happened from what's been believed for so long that if feels real even without evidence. That's what folklore does when it lasts. It fills the air until absence starts to act like fact.

The people who live closest to the hill don't try to explain it. They farm their land and speak of the castle like they speak of weather as something that merely exists, unpredictable but ordinary. Children are told not to play near the path that leads to the castle after dark. Farmers say the soil near the ruins never yields the same as the fields beyond. It sounds like superstition, but that's how communities mark uneasy ground.

Cachtice Castle carries a quiet truth about story and memory. A tale that strong doesn't stay in the mouth of the teller; it sinks into the land that held it. The stones keep more than structure. They keep centuries of fascination, judgment, and regret. Whatever still lingers of Elizabeth Bathory is bound up in that landscape—a place that listens and remembers, whispering through its cracks until it builds fear.

## THE WORK

The legend of Elizabeth Bathory was never only about blood. It's about how power unsettles people, and how quickly strength turns into sin once it belongs to the wrong person. The charges against her acted like a spell cast by a whole country: they named her, feared her, trapped her, and kept repeating her name until fear hardened into myth. In that way her punishment didn't end with death. It kept working through every retelling that used a woman's authority as proof of guilt.

For anyone who practices magic, her story is a lesson in containment. It shows what happens when power is seen without understanding, when visibility becomes exposure instead of recognition. To move through the world intact, you have to learn what she never could—to hold your boundaries so that attention can't drain you. There's quiet spellwork for this kind of steadiness. It doesn't hide you. It centers you, so what people see doesn't reach past the surface.

To begin, work with reflection, both literal and otherwise. Hold a mirror until it shows you clearly, without distortion. See yourself as neither spectacle nor disguise. Brush a little oil along its edge. That's not only for ceremony; it's a physical reminder that boundaries need tending. The mirror becomes a tool for control reclaimed. Light comes in, but projection goes back out. Keep it near your door or workspace to act as a filter. It lets the world see what you choose to show and keeps the rest quiet. That's not hiding. That's standing your ground.

The same rule applies to the unseen mirror you carry inside you. Each time you prepare to be visible when you teach, perform, or speak, you decide how much of yourself crosses that line. The breath you take before beginning, the quiet naming of your intention, works the way any spell does. It says, *This is my reflection. This is my limit.* When the work is done, you release it with the same care. You wash it off with salt, with prayer, or with stillness, so nothing heavy clings.

Bathory's story warns what happens when reflection turns to obsession, when the mirror commands instead of protects. The answer is awareness— knowing where your energy starts and ends. That isn't defensive magic. It's balance.

This lesson reaches beyond history. The myth of the Blood Countess still teaches who may hold power and how they're expected to behave once they do. Every time her story is told as horror, it repeats the idea that ambition in a woman must end in punishment. Reading it as folklore breaks that pattern. It lets you see the spell and choose not to repeat it.

In the end, every story about control is also a story about choice. The same wind that moves through Cachtice's ruins moves through all our stories, reminding us that strength sealed away becomes myth, but strength practiced with awareness becomes legacy. When the world calls you dangerous, ask yourself if danger is just another word for having a threatening presence. Then keep working—not to prove them wrong, but to stay whole while they decide what to name you.

# THE LADY IN WHITE

Every town has a stretch of road that feels different after dark. The pavement narrows, the trees lean too close, and the quiet between the headlights and the treeline begins to vibrate. On nights like that, you understand why people tell stories. Somewhere near a bend in the road, or at the edge of a bridge, someone always swears they saw her—a woman in a long white dress, standing still at the shoulder as if she'd been waiting for centuries. Drivers describe the same moment of unease: they pass, glance back, and she's gone. No sound, no scream, no trace but the feeling that they witnessed something meant for them and also meant for everyone.

These encounters rarely reach newspapers, but they travel mouth to mouth and stay fixed in the landscape. The Lady in White is not a single ghost; she's a pattern that repeats itself in every culture that's ever lost a woman to grief. Depending on where the story lands, she takes on a name and a place. In Mexico and the American Southwest she's *La Llorona*—the weeping woman who walks the riverbanks searching for her drowned children. In Chicago she's Resurrection Mary, forever walking toward the gates of a cemetery she can't quite enter. In Ireland she becomes the Banshee, whose cry comes before death and gives families time to ready their sorrow. The details change in these stories: the accent, the setting, but the structure is the same. A woman suffers a loss society never let her resolve. Death arrives, but peace does not.

The reason these tales survive has less to do with fear and more to do with recognition. They describe grief that never found language, sorrow denied until it turned into movement. The Lady in White keeps walking because no one else finished the ritual. She lives where mourning stopped too soon.

Most people who claim to have seen her don't talk about terror. They talk about silence. A calm so thick it presses on the skin, a chill that feels less like weather and more like empathy. The moment stretches, and for that instant the living and the dead seem to share the same air. That's why these stories stick around. They speak to the part of us that knows what it is to be unseen and still waiting to be acknowledged.

Communities keep her legend alive not only by fear but by duty. A story like this becomes a kind of moral boundary: a reminder to drive slower, to respect certain hours of night, to remember the names of the lost. When the Lady in White appears, she is not there to harm. She's there to make people notice—the road, the danger, the memory of what happens when compassion arrives too late.

The image endures because it touches something older than any one haunting. Every culture that pictures her in white understands that color not as purity but as exposure—the brightness of the image, the last flash before she disappears again. She is grief made visible, and every sighting is a form of recognition. When she appears, the living pause long enough to remember that some stories never stop moving because the mourning never stopped either.

## THE HISTORY

Across centuries and continents, the details change with the landscape, but the heart of the story stays the same whether it is an unresolved death tied to love, betrayal, or motherhood. That consistency gives folklorists their first clue that these women aren't isolated ghosts. They're a shared language. They show what happens when a community refuses to acknowledge its own grief.

One of the best-known is *La Llorona,* the Weeping Woman. Her story moves through nearly every Spanish-speaking household, often told to children before they're old enough to understand it. A woman, usually named María, falls in love with a man above her station. When he leaves her or denies their children, her despair hardens into rage. She drowns the children in a river, sees what she's done, and dies, sometimes by her own hand, sometimes by punishment. After death she walks the waterways crying for the children she can't find. Her wail is said to come before disaster, a sound that warns of floods, accidents, or sudden loss.

Parents use the tale to keep children away from the water, but it runs deeper than discipline. It speaks to grief that has no safe place. Long before colonization, the Aztec goddess Cihuacóatl was said to wander the night mourning her children—a divine guardian of mothers who died in childbirth. After Catholic missionaries reshaped Indigenous belief, that figure became a sinner instead of a saint. Sacred mourning turned into a curse. *La Llorona* carries both legacies still: holy sorrow and moral warning, a woman punished for loving too deeply and for mourning too loudly.

In the United States, the same figure took a new shape. *Resurrection Mary* belongs to the south side of Chicago. Her story started in the 1930s when drivers along Archer Avenue began reporting a young woman in a white dress walking alone near Resurrection Cemetery. Some stopped to offer her a ride. She asked to go toward the gates, but before the car reached them, she disappeared. Others said they saw her pressing her hands against the iron bars, leaving prints that later looked burned into the metal. The witnesses changed over time: a taxi driver, a night guard, a ballroom patron, but the pattern remained. A girl out dancing dies in an accident and spends forever trying to get home.

Unlike *La Llorona,* Mary isn't angry. She doesn't chase. She doesn't cry. Her haunting is repetition without malice. She moves through the same stretch of road the way a dream returns to one image and reminds whoever sees her that some departures aren't permanent. That quietness is what keeps her believable. She behaves like a memory, not a threat. People still leave flowers near the spot where she appears because her presence feels mournful, not dangerous.

Older than both is the Banshee of Irish lore, whose cry runs through Gaelic stories as both terror and warning. The word comes from *bean sídhe*—woman of the fairy mound—linking her to ancient burial ground. She appears when someone from a certain family line is about to die. Her wail doesn't cause the death; it tells that it's coming. The sound is said to be high and thin, human enough to raise the hairs on the neck. In some tales she's young and pale, in others old and gray, but always in white or gray—the color of death shrouds and the river stones where women once washed burial linens.

In earlier centuries, professional keeners, women who sang at funerals to voice grief for the whole community, did the same work among the living. When that custom faded, folklore turned the role into the supernatural. The Banshee became grief itself, a reminder that mourning is duty, not indulgence. When her cry is heard, families pray and ready the house, knowing death is near but not yet through the door.

Each of these women carries the same burden. They keep the line between life and death honest. Where religion tries to comfort by closing the wound, folklore insists on looking at it. *La Llorona, Resurrection Mary,* and the Banshee all demand witness for pain that institutions prefer to hide. That's why their stories keep being told. They're the emotional infrastructure of a community. They're ghosts doing public service.

Outside the famous names, women in white walk almost every landscape. In the Philippines, the White Lady of Balete Drive appears to drivers traveling alone after dark. In Portugal, the *Dama Branca* steps from fog to turn wanderers around before danger finds them. In Japan and Korea, pale women haunt bridges and riversides, echoing the belief that water remembers sorrow. In much of Southeast Asia, their stories tie to betrayal or domestic violence, turning private tragedy into public warning.

The color white ties all these stories together. Across much of Asia and Africa it marks mourning. In Europe it marks burial. It's the color of crossing over and represents the space between life and death, presence and absence. The white dress isn't a costume. It's ritual clothing that shows the wearer has crossed over but won't disappear. It makes her visible enough to be remembered and distant enough to stay sacred.

In every version, the Lady in White stands at thresholds like bridges, roads, rivers, graveyards—all the places where the border between worlds thins. She represents unfinished crossings, whether emotional, moral, or spiritual. That's why she waits near water or at a bend in the road. Those are the landscapes that mirror human uncertainty. When people see her, they're witnessing more than a ghost. They're seeing the outline of unresolved feeling still moving through their own towns.

Taken together, these stories form a map of grief. They teach that mourning has its own order, and when that order breaks, when the dead go unacknowledged or the living are told to move on too soon, the loss doesn't fade. It shifts. It takes shape. It waits by the roadside until someone slows down enough to notice. The Lady in White is that pause made visible—the shape of silence we keep passing by.

## THE MAGIC

The Lady in White isn't one ghost. She's a working symbol, a pattern of energy that crosses borders and belief systems. In every version of her story she stands for grief that never found its full voice. What keeps her moving isn't revenge, it's imbalance. From a magical point of view, she is what happens when mourning doesn't finish, when the ritual stops before the wound closes. That's why she shows up everywhere, in every language, wherever people have lost something they weren't allowed to grieve.

In the language of spirit work, that kind of presence is called unrested energy. It isn't the same as a haunting, and it isn't a soul asking to be saved. It's what remains when experience outlives its body. It lingers where an ending went unfinished: by a river where children drowned, at a crossroads where someone never made it home, at a door where death came and no one said goodbye. The Lady in White isn't one woman. She's the form that energy takes when it needs to be seen.

In most tellings she's tied to three conditions. The first is a death that wasn't mourned right—a body buried in haste or without prayer. The second is grief that was silenced, punished, or shamed into secrecy. The third is a threshold like a bridge, road, or water— some place where movement stopped and something didn't get completed. These conditions repeat so clearly they might as well be the steps of a spell. The ghost becomes a kind of equation: loss without ritual, pain without witness, memory without rest.

When you work with ancestors or open yourself to spirit communication, you'll meet this energy. It feels heavier than air. It sits behind the ribs like a sigh that won't finish. In ritual, it may show as a shadow in a mirror, a sudden weight in the room, or a name spoken that you didn't call. It doesn't frighten. It simply arrives when the door's already open, drawn to anything that carries its same tone. That's why workers who carry unresolved grief tend to meet it first. Energy recognizes its own reflection.

From a practitioner's view, the Lady in White isn't a threat. She's a messenger. She points to where mourning is past due. In ancestor work, she often appears to those who've inherited silence with the stories families never told, the miscarriages or sicknesses never named, the violences buried instead of confessed. In community work, she can show up as a run of accidents or unrest circling one place, waiting for acknowledgment. She doesn't come asking for attention herself. She comes to make sure the grief beneath her story is finally seen.

When this kind of energy enters ritual space, it calls for steadiness, not fear. The worker's task is to decide whether it belongs to personal lineage or to the wider collective. If it feels local like something in the same room or the land you're on, you treat it as a guest. Light a candle, speak aloud that it's been seen, and invite it to rest in peace. If it feels ancestral or emotional—something that answers your own losses, you meet it with cleansing, not conversation. Wash your hands in salt water, cover the mirrors, and remind yourself that recognition isn't the same as ownership. That distinction keeps the living from carrying what the dead were meant to finish.

The Lady in White also teaches a kind of magical courtesy. You don't summon grief for display. You don't call the dead to prove a point. You make room for what was neglected, then you close it. In Latin American and Filipino practice, many workers keep a candle and a cup of water on the altar for unnamed spirits. It's not necessarily to feed them, but to honor what's been forgotten. As we've already talked about, in Appalachian and Irish homes, mirrors are turned to the wall during mourning so the spirit of the newly dead doesn't mistake its reflection for invitation. In hoodoo, that same rule appears in laying grief at a crossroads to give sorrow a road to travel instead of a house to haunt.

All these customs follow the same law: grief must be given direction. Left unacknowledged, she becomes the Lady in White. When she appears, meet her with recognition, not fear. Say aloud that you see her. Thank her for carrying the grief that no one else could face. Then walk away. That simple act releases her from repetition and keeps you from joining her walk.

For those who work closely with spirit, remember that these figures aren't dangerous in the way stories claim. They feel heavy because they hold history. The unease people feel around them comes from meeting that weight. Like a tuning fork that vibrates to its own pitch, the body responds when it nears unresolved grief. The goal isn't to block that vibration but to understand it. Awareness is protection.

Magically speaking, the Lady in White is a mirror for emotion that hasn't been resolved. When she weeps, she reflects collective sorrow that's been denied. When she lures travelers from the road, she points to paths that were never safe to begin with. When she stands silent at the edge of a field, she marks the place where something was buried too quickly. Every telling of her story is what makes the living face their unfinished mourning.

That's why she never leaves folklore. Each retelling renews her. Every time her name is spoken, her purpose begins again. She isn't here to frighten anyone. She's doing the work people avoid—remembering. In that way she's less ghost than guardian. The places she lingers aren't cursed; they're sanctified by her witness. When the living learn to honor grief before it hardens into legend, she'll stop walking. Until then she'll keep her place at the roadside, patient and visible, reminding whoever looks her way that nothing truly rests until it's been seen and given a resolution.

## THE SIGNS

Every region has a road people avoid after dark. It looks harmless enough in daylight such as two lanes of cracked asphalt edged with trees and the smell of water nearby. But when the sun goes down, the air thickens. The wind stops moving. Headlights feel too small. The silence behind the car stretches longer than it should. In almost every town, someone can name that road. They know what waits there. They might not believe in ghosts, but they believe in that one.

These are the places where the Lady in White keeps working. The names change, but the landmarks stay the same—a bridge where wrecks repeat, a curve lined with roadside crosses, a field where fog never lifts. Drivers tell the same story: a figure ahead, a flash of white at the shoulder, an ache that rises in the chest. The rest follows its pattern. They slow down, look back, and she's gone. What stays isn't her image but the feeling that something was recognized. Even the ones who laugh at ghost tales still check the rearview mirror twice.

White Rock Lake in Dallas has been telling that story for generations. Since the 1940s, drivers have stopped for a soaking-wet woman who asks for a ride home. Her dress clings to her, her hair drips with water, and her voice is polite. When they reach the address she gives, the seat beside them is empty. The house belongs to her parents, or so the story goes, and they tell the driver their daughter drowned years ago. The details change each decade, but the feeling never does. It's always about a stranger trying to finish a trip that death cut short.

Across the country in Connecticut, Union Cemetery has its own Lady. She doesn't wait for rides; she walks straight across the road. Some drivers swerve and crash. Others say she passes through the car like a cold wave. People have been trying to photograph her for years. One man said he caught her, showing a streak of light between the stones. But the picture didn't prove much. What lasted was the habit locals picked up: easing off the gas when headlights touch the cemetery wall. That pause says more than the photo ever did.

In the Philippines, the White Lady of Balete Drive is warning more than witness. Taxi drivers talk about her the way sailors talk about storms—as fact. They see her in mirrors, sitting silent in the back seat, or as a pale shape behind the shoulder. Wrecks happen more often on that stretch than anywhere nearby, and no one asks for proof. It isn't fear that keeps people off the road after dark. It's respect. The haunting works as a way to mark that a woman died there, and that the violence done to her still asks to be remembered.

What ties these sightings together is how steady they are. The women never reach home. The drivers never find answers. The stories never end. They loop, as if each telling keeps the energy moving, stopping it from falling into silence. The repetition is the point. It keeps the wound from closing completely. Every person who repeats the story is, in some small way, keeping vigil.

Listen closely and you can hear how these legends change the ground they rest on. The road becomes more than geography; it turns into a shrine disguised as infrastructure. People drive slower. They light candles after accidents. They leave flowers on the guardrail. The community learns to act as if the haunting proves something sacred. Whether anyone believes the ghost is beside the point. The behavior itself is the ritual.

Witnesses rarely talk about terror. They talk about the unease of the moment when the line between the living and the dead thins enough to feel it. They mention how the air got heavy, how silence seemed to wait, how voices felt too loud afterward. That reaction doesn't come from fear of harm. It comes from knowing they'd felt a ghost. The body knows what the mind avoids. Old grief can feel more like an atmosphere than an event. Some places still carry it thick in the air.

You can see that awareness in small gestures. A driver turns down the radio without knowing why. A walker steps aside on an empty road. Someone slows the car to a crawl when fog rises from the ditch. These reflexes are inherited from centuries of folklore. The living adjust to the presence of the dead, whether they believe in them or not. The Lady in White is part of that contract. She keeps the roads honest.

What makes these stories powerful is that they don't resolve. No one frees the ghost, and no one proves she existed. The haunting stays unfinished, like the grief it represents. People touched by it often change small things afterward—they drive more carefully, call someone they miss, leave a flower on a stranger's grave. They may not connect those acts to what they saw, but the impulse comes from the same place. The Lady in White doesn't haunt to scare. She haunts to remind. She stands where something went wrong and waits until someone finally sees it.

That's why these stories are told over and over again. They don't chase the ghosts away. They remind the living what's still unfinished. The fear fades, but the memory doesn't, and for a moment the world feels steady again.

## THE WORK

The Lady in White isn't a ghost that fades with time. She's memory that won't stay buried. Every version of her story begins with grief that got quieted and ends with the living having to face what they looked away from. She isn't there to scare anyone. She's there to finish what was left undone.

In magic, she teaches about boundaries—how energy moves when mourning hasn't finished, and how the living can meet it without being pulled under. Protection isn't about closing yourself off; it's about staying open without getting drained. When you pass a place that feels heavy with her don't try to clear it. Just nod to it. Treat it the way you would a stranger carrying hard news: with respect and a little space. That small act is a kind of spell. It tells whatever lingers that you understand why it's still there and that it doesn't need to follow you home.

The same rule works for grief that lives inside us. When you sit with sorrow, your own or somebody else's, you're walking the same road she walks. The boundary you build isn't made from fear; it's made from clarity. Salt and water. Prayer and breath. Those are the oldest tools we have for giving back what isn't ours to keep. After you've listened to someone's pain, wash your hands and say the words we were never taught: *This grief is not mine to keep.* It's plain language, but plain language closes the circle.

Some people think spellwork means control—commands to the universe, bargains with spirits. The Lady in White shows the opposite. Her work is consent. The haunting lasts only while it's ignored. The moment someone meets her eyes and sees what she's carrying, balance starts to return. That's why flowers and candles appear wherever she's seen. Even folks who don't believe still feel that pull to set something right. Those offerings aren't superstition. They're the oldest kind of folk magic—grief turned into care.

For anyone who works with the dead, she's a reminder that not every ghost belongs to you and not every sorrow is yours to fix. The living often mistake empathy for duty. But empathy is a bridge, not a home. When the weight of collective mourning moves through a room, you can honor it without taking it on. Light one white candle just as a ritual of honor. Let it burn while you name the losses that shaped your people: the forgotten women, the unburied children, the unnamed dead. When the flame goes out, open a window and let the smoke leave. That's how you end the work cleanly.

The Lady in White teaches that magic and mourning run on the same current. Both ask for attention. Both need time. Both fall apart when rushed. She keeps walking because people still treat grief like a mistake instead of a season. Her story keeps showing up until someone listens all the way through.

So when the road curves and you see her in your headlights, don't be afraid. Slow down. Breathe once for yourself and once for whatever she's carrying. You don't need to stop, and you don't need to look away. Seeing her is enough. That brief moment of awareness does what every good ritual does—it connects the living and the dead for just long enough to make peace, then lets both move on.

She'll keep walking because the world still has grief left to name. That's her work. Ours is to pay attention when we see her and to remember what she stands for. Grief doesn't go away just because we stop talking about it. It waits until someone's ready to face it. That's all she's ever asked us to do. To see her.

# THE DYBBUK BOX

In every antique shop there's at least one box you don't want to touch. The wood seems to breathe. The hinges resist. The air around it smells faintly of something sweet that should have faded long ago. People who have owned boxes like these say they hum in quiet rooms and leave the taste of metal in the mouth. The one that became famous is called the Dybbuk Box. It's a small wine cabinet said to hold a restless spirit sealed inside.

The story began simply. A man found the cabinet, bought it, and decided to sell it online. In the listing he called it a Dybbuk Box and claimed it once belonged to a Holocaust survivor who used it to trap a spirit. He warned that every person who had owned it suffered misfortune. Illness. Accidents. Bad dreams. The story spread quickly. Within weeks the box was famous, moving from one owner to another as though it were alive. Television crews filmed it. A horror movie borrowed its name. A museum displayed it behind glass. People came to see it the way you visit a grave that never stays quiet.

Later the seller admitted the tale was fiction. The box had never held a spirit. The wax that sealed it was only for show. The story about survivors, rabbis, and rituals was built from borrowed sorrow and shaped into something meant to scare. But by the time the truth came out, it didn't matter. The story already had a life of its own. People who touched the box still claimed to dream strange dreams. They heard tapping on the walls. They felt cold air in rooms with no windows. They woke with a pressure on their chest that lifted only when they left the house. What began as a lie started to behave like folklore.

That is how objects become haunted. Not through spirits that live inside them but through the meaning we give them. The Dybbuk Box became a vessel for everything people feared but could not name. Grief that would not leave. Guilt that would not fade. Memory that refused to stay buried. Whether the story was real or not stopped mattering. What mattered was how people responded to it and how belief filled the cracks that wood and wax could not.

The Dybbuk Box is not the oldest haunted object and it won't be the last. It shows how quickly an ordinary thing can turn sacred once it becomes a container for fear. Some say the box hums because it holds a spirit. Others say it hums because it holds our attention. What is certain is that people believed it, and belief alone was enough to make it work.

## THE HISTORY

To understand the Dybbuk Box, you have to go back to the word that gave it power. In Jewish folklore, a dybbuk is not a ghost that drifts through walls or rattles doors. It is a soul that clings to the living when something in its story has not been settled. The word comes from the Hebrew *dābaq*, which means "to cling." That is the heart of it—a displaced soul attaching itself to a person instead of a place, trying to find rest through someone else's breath.

The earliest mentions appear in writings from the sixteenth to eighteenth centuries, most from Eastern

Europe where Jewish communities lived under constant threat. Pogroms, exile, and forced conversion were common. The world was uncertain, and so were the dead. Mystical teachings from that time, especially those tied to Rabbi Isaac Luria of Safed, taught that souls return through *gilgul*, or transmigration. But not all of them return clean. When a person dies with guilt unspoken, injustice unresolved, or violence unanswered, that soul can resist moving on. It may cling to someone living, drawn to a heart or a house that feels familiar.

In those stories, possession is not punishment. It is a wound carried forward. The person afflicted might speak in another's voice or remember things they never saw. The dybbuk doesn't wander without aim. It seeks repair. Exorcism in that tradition is not a fight between good and evil. It is an act of reconciliation. A rabbi or mystic questions the spirit, asks its name, and finds what must be released. When the truth is spoken and the wrong is forgiven, the dybbuk can leave. The work ends not in spectacle but in stillness.

By the nineteenth century, dybbuks had become part of everyday folklore. They turned up in village tales and traveling plays, most of them stories of love and loss. The best known was *The Dybbuk, or Between Two Worlds,* written in 1914 by S. Ansky. In that play, a young woman named Leah is taken over by the spirit of her dead lover after her father forbids their marriage. The spirit isn't evil. It's desperate. What speaks through Leah's voice is grief that never found words. Audiences wept, not from fear but from recognition. The play carried the same truth the old mystics had taught. Possession is another word for mourning that hasn't finished its work.

The modern Dybbuk Box borrowed the name but not the meaning. The box that appeared on the internet in the early 2000s had nothing to do with theology or mysticism. Its story was written for a time that loves to turn fear into entertainment. Still, the public treated it like a real haunting. They asked the same questions, repeated the same words, and gave their energy to the idea until it began to behave like truth.

That is how folklore travels—from synagogue to stage to screen to a secondhand cabinet listed for sale. The names might change, but the fear doesn't.

## THE MAGIC

The idea of the dybbuk has lasted because it gives people a name for something they already know. It explains the weight that sits on a person when grief refuses to move. In Jewish mysticism, a dybbuk isn't a monster from outside. It's a soul in crisis, tied to the living by unfinished work. When that idea moved into folklore, it became a way to talk about the times when pain outlives memory.

The Dybbuk Box carries that same function even

though its story was made up. The box was never part of Jewish ritual. No text ever mentioned trapping a spirit in furniture. Still, the image made sense to a modern audience. The world is full of things that hold memory such as photographs, heirlooms, and family homes. A wooden box that could store sorrow felt believable. That's why people touched it and said they felt sick, or dreamed in strange voices, or smelled flowers that weren't there. It gave them a place to set what they didn't understand.

In folklore, that's the work of magic. It turns what can't be seen into something that can be handled. A story about a haunted box is easier to face than the truth that grief and history often follow us without a face. Objects become vessels for what we can't name. Once people believe that, it starts to act like ritual. Every time the box was opened or filmed or passed to another owner, it repeated the same pattern of invitation, fear, and release. That pattern built its own kind of charge.

The Dybbuk Box became a mirror for the old dybbuk stories. It didn't hold a soul. It held attention. People who stood near it said their chest felt heavy or their skin crawled. The box didn't cause that. Recognition did. The body knows when it stands near something that's been filled with too much emotion.

That's why the box still draws people. It's a lesson disguised as a curse. It shows how belief itself can move power through ordinary things. The same current that gives life to prayer can also give life to fear. Once set in motion, both move through word, through air, through touch. The only difference is what they do once they reach you.

## THE SIGNS

Cursed objects follow a familiar pattern. Something is found, a warning is ignored, and the story that follows is told again and again until it grows larger than the object itself. The Dybbuk Box fits that pattern exactly. It began as one man's fiction and became a collection of testimonies through letters, videos, and online posts that all described the same uneasy feeling. Lights flicker, glass breaks, dreams repeat. The words change, but the signs stay the same. People who have never met describe the same reactions because belief has a way of joining separate experiences until they begin to line up.

When enough people believe in a thing, it starts to behave like magic. A person who touches an object already called cursed carries that story into the room with them. Their body responds to what their mind has accepted. The air feels colder, the pulse quickens, and the imagination fills in what the senses can't explain. That isn't fraud; it's what people do when pattern meets expectation. Folklore uses repetition to keep old lessons alive. When an object is said to hold danger, it teaches caution even when no true curse is present. The story of the Dybbuk Box keeps working because it lives in the space between fear and suggestion, and people still visit that space willingly.

Over time, other boxes began appearing online: some sealed with wax, some tied with string, all claiming to be part of the same story. The sellers may not have believed what they were offering, but the buyers often did. They filmed themselves breaking the seals, hoping to catch proof of a haunting, and in doing so they created a new ritual. Once the wax broke and the story was spoken aloud, the pattern repeated itself. The room grew quiet, the expectation took root, and the belief renewed the legend without anyone needing to invent more.

Belief doesn't need a single object to survive. It spreads through imitation. When people began opening these boxes on social media, the practice traveled faster than any folktale could have spread by word of mouth. Viewers said they felt dizzy or sick, and some heard whispers through their phones. It wasn't the sound that mattered but the repetition. The more people watched, the stronger the charge became. That is how a modern haunting works by depending on the attention people give it.

There are still stories of people who bring these boxes home and notice the air grow heavy. Cats avoid certain rooms, clocks stop, and faint smells of perfume or smoke appear and disappear. Most of the time the unease fades once the object is moved or cleaned, but what stays behind is the sense that belief leaves residue. Objects that draw attention take on energy, and it hardly matters whether that energy comes from spirits or from people. It feels the same either way.

The Dybbuk Box taught a new generation something old workers already knew. An object can hold the memory of what it's been given. In conjure work a charm is fed. In European practice relics become holy through touch. In every culture, intention leaves a trace. The lesson isn't to fear the object but to understand that belief, once focused, becomes part of the inner workings of what people experience.

## THE WORK

The Dybbuk Box reminds us that not every haunting comes from the dead. Some are born from too much human attention. A story that has been fed too long starts to move on its own. That is what happened here. What began as invention became a vessel for memory, fear, and fascination. The story grew past the object because people kept touching it, talking about it, and carrying it forward. Every retelling turned belief into quiet ritual.

In most magical systems, attention is a kind of offering. Whatever we look at with focus begins to grow. That is why experienced workers learn restraint. You do not stare too long at what you fear, and you do not repeat another person's curse unless you are ready to carry it yourself. Words keep working as long as someone continues to speak them. The Dybbuk Box proves the rule that belief without boundaries becomes a living thing.

There is another lesson here, and it's older than the internet. Every community has objects that hold memory. Some sit on altars, some stay in drawers, and some pass through families until no one remembers where they came from. The respectful thing is not to call them cursed but to ask why they were kept. In Jewish homes, written prayers and amulets hold what is too heavy to carry unguarded. In hoodoo, that burden is often bound into a jar or charm so that energy can rest instead of wander. A haunted object is what happens when that kind of work is done without intention.

The cure is the same as it has always been: naming and release. When something feels charged or unsettled, you treat it the same way you would treat grief that has been left too long unspoken. Bring it into the light, say what it is, and decide whether it belongs to you. If it does, cleanse it. If it doesn't, return it. Simple tools like salt, smoke, water, or prayer have always been enough. The strength doesn't come from the ingredients. It comes from the decision to close what has been left open.

If you ever find yourself holding an object that feels

unsettled or have heavy energy, treat it the same way you'd treat a house that's seen too much argument. Begin with a bowl of cool water and a pinch of salt. Stir it once clockwise and once counterclockwise, then set the bowl beside the object. Say quietly, *"What clings without cause, find rest. What follows without name, find peace."* Leave the bowl there overnight. In the morning, pour the water into the earth, never down the drain. The act isn't meant to banish. It's meant to release what was never yours to keep.

The Dybbuk Box doesn't teach fear of spirits. It teaches responsibility for story. The danger was never in the wood or the wax. It was in how easily imagination replaced understanding. Folklore is meant to explain the unknown, not invent it for profit. When fear turns into entertainment, the line between witness and participant disappears. What follows is confusion—a haunting not of spirit, but of meaning.

Real magic restores order. It gathers what has scattered and gives it shape again. If something has attached to you, or if you've carried a weight that isn't yours, the first step is stillness. Breathe. Remember who you are. Refuse to host what doesn't belong. In that clarity, the energy finds its own way home.

The Dybbuk Box will keep traveling because people need the story it carries. It warns that grief and guilt left unspoken will always find a voice. It reminds us that belief can build as easily as it can destroy. When an object feels heavy, listen before deciding what to call it. Most of the time it isn't a curse. It's a memory that just wants someone to acknowledge it.

# CONCLUSION

The stories in this first volume began as sound—thirty minutes of telling stories to anyone drawn to the eerie and the unknown. Once they were gathered on the page, it was clear what they'd really been about all along. These aren't ghost stories. They're records of how people live with things they can't quite explain. Every superstition, every haunting, and every bit of magic is how people manage what they don't understand.

Season One of *The Feral Folklorist* podcast followed that path through crossroads and kitchens, graveyards and spooky roads. The places changed, but the reason for telling them never did. Folk belief isn't just faith. It's the work people do to stay balanced between what they can see and what they can't. It's how they keep a sense of order when reason runs short. A charm on the wall, salt at the door, or a candle burning through the night aren't decorations. They're upkeep.

What ties these stories together is the same rule that guides any magical worker or folklorist: pay attention, respect the beliefs, and don't touch what you don't understand. Every legend in these pages follows that rule. The Devil at the crossroads, the Greenbrier ghost, Marie Laveau's tomb, the mirrors at the Myrtles—they all carry the same truth. The dead don't always want revenge. Most of the time they just want the living to help finish what they started.

These stories stay alive because they're honest about need. They show that fear and faith often grow from the same soil, and that magic and survival are sometimes the same work done with different words. If you listen long enough, you'll hear that pattern everywhere: in a bottle tree rattling in the wind, in a house that goes quiet before a death, in a patch of ground that remembers what was buried there. Folklore doesn't vanish. It waits for someone to notice again.

Belief is a different experience for different people. Sometimes it shows up as prayer. Sometimes as an old habit. Sometimes as a story told so often it starts to sound like fact. Folklore isn't just nostalgia. It's a witness. The living listen. The dead keep talking. And somewhere between them is the truth that keeps us steady.

The next volume will start from here with new places, new hauntings, new ways the old rules still show up when we need them. None of this ends. The stories change shape, but they don't disappear. They wait for the next listener, the next worker, the next person willing to sit with the strange long enough to learn from it.

*Papa Coll*